*Dedicated to
Scott Spiegel,
who gave me the greatest gift,
a career*

FROM DUSK TILL DAWN
Screenplay by
Quentin Tarantino

Story by Robert Kurtzman

faber and faber
LONDON · BOSTON

First published in 1996
by Faber and Faber Limited
3 Queen Square London WCIN 3AU
Open market edition first published in 1996
This UK paperback edition first published in 1996

Photoset by Parker Typesetting Service, Leicester
Printed in England by Clays Ltd, St Ives plc

A CIP record for this book
is available from the British Library
ISBN 0–571–19007–3

2 4 6 8 10 9 7 5 3 1

CONTENTS

FOREWORD

A true vampire is, at its cold heart, indiscriminate. It goes where its needs take it, the necks of the high-born and the low deemed equally valuable. As long as there's a pulse, they're to the purpose. Little wonder then that the vampire has experienced a return to favour: it shares with our culture the instinct of the scavenger. Impurity is the mode of the moment; we seek out and celebrate art that revels in its own promiscuity, taking vigour from whatever veins the artist lays his or her hungry eye upon.

All of which makes Quentin Tarantino fit for induction into the league of the living dead at his earliest convenience, for there's surely nobody working in the heat of the popular gaze who has so successfully shed, mingled, and prospered upon blood from such a variety of sources. In his neo-noirs, *Reservoir Dogs*, *True Romance*, and *Pulp Fiction*, low comedy, high melodrama, hip tunes, and mesmeric violence are fused by the sheer force of his storytelling, his characters as addicted to the ephemeral pleasures of a hamburger or their own chatter as their creator. It's an infectious delight. Once bitten, we're laughing along with Quentin's happy monsters as they taunt, torment, and slaughter one another.

From Dusk Till Dawn opens in this same terrain: a place where violence is arbitrary and cruelty more likely to evoke guilty laughter than censure. But the road trip Quentin's characters (good, bad, confused, and simply crazy) undertake soon leads them astray, and halfway through the movie Quentin the screenwriter, Quentin the actor, and director Robert Rodriguez get to play a very different set of variations. The thriller grows fangs, the bullets are passed over in favour of holy water, and we're in the midst of a high-octane vampire flick.

This is not, need I say, the *fin de siècle* world conjured by a sensualist like Anne Rice, in which the melancholy undead brood and swoon in one another's arms. Tarantino and Rodriguez have created a nest of banshee vampires stripped of poetry or doubt. Nor do they seem to be an endangered species. They swarm over the screen in screeching waves of virulent appetite, their horde thinned only at terrible cost to our dubious heroes.

Rodriguez stages these action scenes in hip, comedic style, the moodier, more realistic tone of the first half of the picture abandoned as the body count grows and the rules of combat become more rococo. If we were disturbed by some of the earlier passages, it was because they had some connection to the context of the *Six O'Clock News*, but once the dance of the vampires begins the carnage becomes so excessive that the grimmest moments seem playful, driven by a mixture of gags and gore that recalls Sam Raimi's *Evil Dead* series.

That's not the only point of reference, of course. This is a vampire flick made by men who know the horror tradition. Peter Cushing, Hammer's great star and (for me, at least) the definitive Van Helsing, gets a nod, so – in the sheer relentlessness of the enemy – do Romero's zombie films, along with pictures by Carpenter and Polanski. There are a host of incidental pleasures besides the grue: a parade of skin-flick sex goddesses, a list speech as sleazy as it is exhaustive, a plethora of state-of-the-screen transformations and resurrections. There's also a complete disregard for the conventional niceties of who survives and who goes down spurting. In truth, it's hard to know which side truly wins the night, but who's counting?

All of this is too much chaotic fun to be frightening, of course. The film doesn't have the patience for anxiety or dread: it wants blood. The spirit of Dracula – urbane, discreet and chilly – has no place at the party Tarantino and Rodriguez are throwing. It's an all-nighter for the vampire babes and their bat-brute lovers; Dracula's Old World manners would be absurdly out of place.

He might be more than a little envious too, seeing Tarantino unapologetically supping from whatever vein suits him. It's a lesson in the modern method, and while the age applauds Quentin, Dracula will have to sulk in his grave awhile. The title of Vampire King is somebody else's for the night.

Clive Barker,
Kauai, Hallowe'en 1995

'I earnestly wish an end would come to this bloody race I am forced to run.'

Countess in Jess Franco's *La Comtesse Noire*

FADE IN:

EXT. LIQUOR STORE – DAY

A convenience store in a Texas suburb. No other businesses surround it.

Close-up: A light switch is flipped on.

The sign on top of the store lights up. It reads: 'Benny's World of Liquor.'

Subtitle appears at bottom of screen:
BIG SPRINGS, TEXAS
109 MILES WEST OF ABILENE
345 MILES EAST OF THE MEXICAN BORDER
A Texas Ranger patrol car pulls into the parking lot and a real live Texas Ranger, Earl McGraw, steps out. McGraw is in full Ranger uniform – button shirt, cowboy hat, boots, mirrored shades, tin star and a Colt revolver on his hip.

It's about an hour and a half before sundown and McGraw is off duty for the day.

The only other car in the parking lot is a 1975 Plymouth (Charley Varrick's car).

INT. BENNY'S WORLD OF LIQUOR – DAY

A young Hawaiian shirt-wearing man named Pete Bottoms sits on a stool behind the counter.

A few customers fiddle about.

A Man wearing a black suit, black tie, and wire-rimmed glasses holds hands with a pretty blonde girl in cut-offs and bare feet. They look through magazines.

Another black-suited man holds hands with a red-headed girl in a prep school uniform. They look through the beer cooler in the back of the store. Both girls are around seventeen.

I

McGraw enters the store.

MCGRAW

Hot goddamn day!

PETE

Haven't felt it a bit. Been inside with the air-conditioner blastin' all day long.

MCGRAW

Not even for lunch?

PETE

I'm by myself today, ate my lunch outta the microwave.

McGraw walks over to the beer cooler, as if it's a nightly ritual (it is), takes out a beer, pops it open and joins Pete by the front counter.

MCGRAW

Jesus Christ man, that microwave food'll kill ya as quick as a bullet. Those burritos are only fit for hippies high on weed. Pull me down a bottle of Jack Daniels. I'm gettin' tanked tonight.

PETE

Whatsamatter?

MCGRAW
(sighs)

Awww, it's just been a shit ass day. Every inch of it hot and miserable. First off, Nadine at the Blue Chip got some sorta sick, so that Mongoloid boy of her's was workin' the grill. That fuckin' idiot don't know rat shit from Rice Krispies. I ate breakfast at nine, was pukin' up pigs in a blanket like a sick dog by ten thirty.

PETE

Isn't there a law or something against retards serving food to the public?

MCGRAW

Well, if there ain't, there sure oughta be. Who knows what goes on inside a Mongoloid's mind?

PETE

You could sue the shit outta her, ya know. That kid belongs under a circus tent, not flippin' burgers. You could own that fucking place.

> MCGRAW

What the hell would I do with that grease pit? Besides, Nadine's got enough of a cross to bear just taking care of that potato head. Then all this Abilene shit happened. You heard about that bank robbery in Abilene, didn't ya?

> PETE

That's all that's been on the box all day. They killed some people, didn't they?

> MCGRAW

Four Rangers, three cops and two civilians. And they took a lady bank teller as a hostage.

Pete doesn't say anything.

They'll probably make a run for the border, which would bring 'em this way. And if we get our hands on those shit asses, we're talkin' payback time. We'll get 'em all right. I gotta piss. I'm gonna use your commode.

> PETE

Knock yourself out.

McGraw downs his last drop of beer, crushes the can and exits into the bathroom.

The black-suited man by the beer cooler turns around and, with the prep school girl in tow, walks rapidly toward Pete. We see that the girl is crying.

> BLACK-SUITED MAN #1
> (*to Pete*)

Do you think I'm fuckin' playing with you, asshole?

Points to the tearful prep school girl.

Do you want this little girl to die?

Pointing to the blonde girl by the other guy.

Or that little girl? Or your bosom buddy with the badge? Or

3

yourself? I don't wanna do it, but I'll turn this fuckin' store into *The Wild Bunch* if I even think you're fuckin' with me.

The two men in black suits are the notorious Abilene bank robbers, Seth and Richard Gecko, 'the Gecko Brothers'. And the other customers are all being held hostage. Seth is the one with the prep school girl. Richard is with the blonde. Everybody speaks low and fast.

PETE

What do you want from me? I did what you said.

SETH

Letting him use your toilet? No store does that.

PETE

He comes in here every day and we bullshit. He's used my toilet a thousand times. If I told him no, he'd know something was up.

SETH

I want that son-of-a-bitch outta here, in his car, and down the road or you can change the name of this place to 'Benny's World of Blood'.

Richard, holding the hand of the terrified girl tightly, leans next to Seth's ear and whispers something. Seth looks at Pete.

Were you giving that pig signals?

> PETE

What? Are you kidding? I didn't do anything!

Richard whispers something else in Seth's ear.

> SETH

He says you were scratching.

> PETE

I wasn't scratching!

> SETH

You callin' him a liar?

Pete controls himself.

> PETE

I'm not calling him a liar, okay? I'm simply saying, if I was scratching, I don't remember scratching, and if I did scratch, it's not because I was signaling the cop, it's because I'm fuckin' scared shitless.

Richard speaks for the first time in a low calm voice to Seth.

> RICHARD

The Ranger's taking a piss. Why don't I just go in there, blow his head off and get outta here.

> PETE

Don't do that! Look, you asked me to act natural, and I'm acting natural – in fact, under the circumstances, I think I ought to get a fuckin' Academy Award for how natural I'm acting. You asked me to get rid of him, I'm doing my best.

> SETH

Yeah, well, your best better get a helluva lot fuckin' better, or you're gonna feel a helluva lot fuckin' worse.

The toilet flushes.

Everybody be cool.

Everybody goes back to what they were doing.

McGraw steps out of the back. He appears to be unaware of the situation.

                         MCGRAW
Yeah, and I'm gonna be right back at it tomorrow. So tonight I'm gonna sit in front of the box and just drink booze. How much is the bottle?

                         PETE
Six-fifty.

Out of nowhere, Richard whips out his .45 automatic and shoots McGraw in the head.

McGraw goes down screaming.

Richard stands over him and shoots him twice more.

Seth charges forward.

                         SETH
                    (*to Richard*)
What the fuck was that about?

                         RICHARD
                   (*in a low monotone*)
He signaled the Ranger.

                         PETE
                     (*hysterical*)
I didn't.
                      (*to Seth*)
You gotta believe me, I didn't.

                         RICHARD
                      (*to Seth*)
When they were talkin', he mouthed the words, 'Help us.'

                         PETE
You fuckin' liar, I didn't say shit!

Richard shoots Pete, who falls down behind the counter.

Seth grabs Richard and throws him up against the wall.

SETH

What the fuck is wrong with you –

RICHARD

Seth, he did it. You were by the beer cooler with your back turned. I was by the magazines, I could see his face. And I saw him mouth:

Richard mouths the words 'Help us'.

While Pete lies on the floor behind the counter bleeding from his bullet wound, he opens his floor safe and pulls out a gun.

Seth releases his brother.

SETH

Start the car.

RICHARD

You believe me, don'tcha?

SETH

Shut up and start the car.

Richard walks away from Seth and crosses the counter . . .

. . . as Pete springs up, gun in hand, and shoots Richard in the shoulder.

Richard falls to his knees, howling.

Both Pete and Seth spray the store with gunfire.

Seth dives down an aisle. He reloads.

Pete ducks behind the counter. He reloads.

Richard has crawled to safety behind an aisle.

The two girls have run out screaming.

(*yelling*)

Richie? You okay?

RICHARD
(*yelling*)

I'm not dead, but I'm definitely shot! I told you that bastard said, 'Help us!'

PETE
(*yelling*)

I never said help us!

SETH
(*yelling*)

Well that don't matter now, 'cause you got about two fuckin'
seconds to live! Richie!

RICHARD
(*yelling*)

Yeah?

SETH
(*yelling*)

When I count three, shoot out the bottles behind him!

RICHARD

Gotcha!

SETH

One . . . Two . . . Three.

The two brothers start firing toward the counter.

They hit the bottles of alcohol on the shelf behind Pete.

*Pete is crouched on the ground as glass, debris and alcohol rain down
on him.*

Seth grabs a roll of paper towels from off a shelf.

Richard keeps firing.

*Seth douses the paper towels with lighter fluid, sets it on fire with his
Zippo, then tosses it.*

The flaming roll of paper towels flies through the air.

The fireball lands behind the counter.

*The entire counter area immediately bursts into flames. Pete screams
from behind the counter.*

Seth smiles to himself and stands.

Richard shakes his head in amusement and stands.

Pete runs out from behind the counter, engulfed in flames, still holding his weapon and firing.

Seth and Richard hit the ground firing their .45s.

Pete, the human torch, falls like a tree into the Hostess Pastry display.

Seth and Richard rise from the rubble.

EXT. BENNY'S WORLD OF LIQUOR – DAY

They exit the store squabbling. The store is bursting into flames.

> SETH

What did I tell you? What did I tell you? Buy the road map and leave.

> RICHARD

What am I supposed to do, Seth? He recognized us.

> SETH

He didn't recognize shit.

Both Seth and Richard stand on opposite sides of the car.

> RICHARD

Seth, I'm telling you, the way he looked at us – you especially – I knew he knew.

They both climb into the car, Seth behind the wheel. Seth starts it up. The souped-up engine roars to life. We can hear Seth mumbling under the motor.

> SETH

Low profile. Do you know what the words 'low profile' mean?

Close-up: Seth's foot punches gas.

The Plymouth tears out of the parking lot backwards, hits the street, and speeds off down the road.

We crane up high to see the car leaving a trail of dust behind it, as the store burns out of control.

TITLE SEQUENCE: *Raunchy, honky-tonk music fills the theatre.*

CUT TO:

EXT. EMMA AND PETE'S GRAVY TRAIN – DAY

Emma and Pete's Gravy Train is a truck stop off of Highway 290.

Subtitle appears at the bottom of the screen:
FORT STOCKTON
238 MILES FROM THE MEXICAN BORDER

INT. EMMA AND PETE'S GRAVY TRAIN – DAY

Emma and Pete's patrons are made up of regulars, truckers, cowboys and road-weary travelers. The camera dollies through the maze of tables, patrons and waitresses.

It stops when it gets to a table occupied by the Fuller Family. The Fullers definitely fall into the road-weary category. The members of the unit consist of the father, Jacob, aged forty-four, an ex-preacher, a good man with rough edges, and his two children. Kate, aged nineteen, is a young beauty who possesses what can only be described as an apple pie sensuality. She is dressed like a nice Christian girl, complete with

10

II

*crucifix. Scott, aged sixteen, is Jacob's Vietnamese adopted son. Scott is
a likable, long-haired kid who wears a T-shirt with the name of the
heavy metal garage band he plays guitar for, Precinct 14. The three of
them are wolfing down a late lunch.*

JABOB

We got about two more hours of daylight left. That'll get us into
El Paso, which is right next to the border. We'll stop at a motel –

SCOTT

Stop? We're not going to actually stop at a motel, are we?

*Scott and Kate speak together, obviously repeating something that
Jacob has said about three hundred times.*

SCOTT/KATE

We've got a Winnebago. We don't need those overpriced roach
havens. We're self-contained.

JACOB

Okay, okay, maybe I was little overzealous, but give me a break. I
just bought it.

Scott and Kate continue the impersonation.

SCOTT

Why, just look at all this. You got your kitchen –

KATE

– you got your microwave –

SCOTT

– you got your sink –

KATE

– you got your shower –

SCOTT

– see this, television!

KATE

Feel this, real wood paneling. That's real wood, too, not that fake stuff.

JACOB

Unless you two wiseacres wanna be introduced to the joys of hitchhiking, what say we drop this?

SCOTT
(*to Kate*)

The truth hurts.

KATE
(*to Scott*)

It's the bitterest of pills.

JACOB

You two ought to start a stand-up act, because you're just wasting your humor on me.

KATE

Ain't it the truth.

SCOTT

Why do you wanna stop?

JACOB

I'm exhausted.

SCOTT

Lie in the back, Dad, I'll drive us into Mexico.

Jacob gives Scott a look that says, 'You aren't touching my new motor home.'

JACOB

I just bet you would. Don't even think about it. Besides, I want to have one night's sleep in an honest-to-goodness bed. The beds in the home are okay, but they're not like a real bed.

KATE

Hey, if we go to a motel, we can swim.

SCOTT

I'll be right back. I'm gonna go to the bathroom.

Scott gets up from the table and walks out back to the restroom.

Jacob and Kate are left alone. There's an awkward moment of silence before . . .

KATE

Dad, when I called the machine to check out our messages there was one from Bethel Baptist. Mr Franklin said he wouldn't permanently replace you until we came back. He said when we come home, if you still feel the same way –

JACOB

That's very nice of Ted, but I'll call him tomorrow and tell him not to bother waiting.

KATE

I didn't want to talk about this in front of Scott because he gets upset. But don't you believe in God anymore?

JACOB

Not enough to be a pastor. Look, I know this is hard on you kids. After Jenny's death, this is probably the last thing you need. But I can't do it any longer. My congregation needs spiritual leadership. Well, they can't get that from me anymore. My faith is gone. To answer your question, yes, I do believe in God. Yes, I do believe in Jesus. But do I love them? No. After Jenny died, I just thought, what's the point?

14

KATE
(*pushing him*)
It's just, all our lives you've been a pastor. For twenty years you've
preached trust in the Lord. And then one day you wake up and say
fuck him?

JACOB
I didn't say fuck him. I'm just not connected anymore.

KATE
That happens, you'll get it back.

JACOB
Kate, give your old man a little credit. Every person who chooses
the service of God as their life's work has something in common. I
don't care if you're a preacher, a priest, a nun, a rabbi or a
Buddhist monk. Many, many times during your life you'll look at
your reflection in the mirror and ask yourself, am I a fool? We've
all done it. I'm not going through a lapse. What I've experienced
is closer to awakening. I'm not trying to shake your faith. I've just
decided not to devote my life to God anymore.

KATE
What do you think Mom would say?

JACOB
Mom's got nothing to say, she's dead.
CUT TO:

Close up: counter bell. A hand slams down on it. Ring.

INT. LOBBY – DEW DROP INN – DAY

*Seth stands at the front desk of the Dew Drop Inn. A standard issue
Texas motel. Richard sits outside in the car. Nobody responds to the bell.
Seth bangs it impatiently five times.*

TEXAS VOICE
(*off-screen*)
Hold your horses!

*An Old-Timer walks through a curtain behind the counter. He's
eating a BBQ rib.*

15

OLD-TIME
(*rough*)

Whatcha want?

SETH

Whatcha think I want, ya mean old bastard? I wanna room.

EXT. COURTYARD — DEW DROP INN — DAY

Richard sits in the car listening to Merle Haggard on the radio. He watches, from his perspective, Seth taking the keys, walking outside and getting into the car. Seth starts it up, and drives them to their room.

RICHARD

Do they have cable?

SETH

No.

RICHARD

Do they have an X-rated channel?

SETH

No.

RICHARD

Do they have a waterbed?

SETH

They don't have anything except four walls and a roof, and that's all we need.

Their car drives up to Room 9, but they park backing up the trunk close to the door.

The two brothers get out of the car.

(*tossing Richard the motel keys*)
Open the door. We gotta do this fast.

Richard opens the door.

Seth goes to the trunk, looks around the courtyard. It's empty.

Close up: key going into the trunk lock, turning.

Trunk POV: Seth looking into the camera.

Seth's POV: A Woman in her late forties is lying scrunched up in the trunk.

She is the hostage bank teller from Abilene. She's stiff, scared and looks an absolute mess.

Don't say a word.

The two brothers, quick as lightening, yank the woman out of the trunk and whisk her into the motel room. Seth closes the trunk, looks around for any Johnny Eye-witnesses, doesn't see any, slams the door.

INT. SETH'S AND RICHARD'S ROOM – DAY

Seth turns from the door, sees the Hostage Woman standing.

                    SETH
You. Plant yourself in that chair.

She sits down in the chair.

                    HOSTAGE
What are you planning on doing with –

                    SETH
– I said plant yourself. Plants don't talk. You wanna get on my good side? Just sit still and don't make a peep.

She shuts up.

Richard slowly takes off his jacket. He winces from his wound.

Let me help you.

He helps him get his jacket off. Richard's white shirt is bloody around the shoulder area. His wound is wrapped up underneath.

How's it feel?

                    RICHARD
How ya think, it hurts like a son-of-a-bitch.

17

Richard goes over to the bed and lies down on it. Seth takes the pillows and stacks them for Richard to prop his back up against.

SETH

I got both rooms on either side of us, so we don't gotta worry about eavesdropping assholes. How's that feel? You okay?

RICHARD

Feels good.

SETH

I'm gonna go get the money.

He heads for the door.

EXT. COURTYARD – MOTEL – DAY

Seth goes into the car, takes out a big suitcase. He scans the perimeter with his eyes, goes back inside.

INT. MOTEL ROOM 9 – DAY

Seth comes back in, lays the suitcase on the bed. Richie has the TV remote control in his hand and he's flipping stations. Seth looks at his watch.

SETH

It's about five o'clock.

(*to Hostage*)

What time does it get dark around here?

HOSTAGE

About seven.

SETH

Good. I'm going towards the border to check things out while it's still daylight, call Carlos and arrange the rendezvous.

RICHARD

Hey, when you talk to him, see if you can arrange a better deal than thirty percent.

SETH

That's their standard deal, brother. They ain't about to change it for us.

RICHARD

Did you even try to negotiate?

SETH

These guys ain't spic firecracker salesmen from Tijuana. They don't even know the meaning of the word barter. You wanna stay in El Ray? You give them thirty percent of your loot. It's scripture. So it is written, so shall it be done. You want sanctuary, you pay the price, and the price is thirty percent.

RICHARD

All I'm saying –

SETH

– this conversation is over.

Richard shrugs and turns back to the TV. Seth turns to the Hostage, grabs a chair and slides it up in front of her.

Now, we need to have a talk. What's your name?

HOSTAGE

Gloria.

He shakes her hand.

19

Hello, Gloria, I'm Seth and that's my brother Richie. Let's cut to the chase. I'm gonna ask you a question and all I want is a yes or no answer. Do you want to live through this?

GLORIA

Yes.

SETH

Good. Then let me explain the house rules. Follow the rules, we'll get along like a house on fire. Rule number one: No noise, no questions. You make a noise . . .

He holds up his .45.

. . . Mr .45 makes a noise. You ask a question, Mr .45 answers it. Now, are you absolutely, positively clear about rule number one?

GLORIA

Yes.

SETH

Rule number two: You do what we say, when we say it. If you don't, see rule number one.

Seth takes the .45, places the barrel next to the woman's cheek. She squirms and shuts her eyes. He pulls back the hammer.

Rule number three: Don't you ever try and fuckin' run on us. 'Cause I got five little friends, and they all run faster'n you can. Got it?

She nods her head 'yes'.

He takes the gun away and replaces the hammer.

Open your eyes.

She does.

Gloria, you hang in there, follow the rules, and don't fuck with us, you'll get out of this alive. I give you my word. Okay?

She nods 'yes'.

Seth rises.

I'll be back in a bit.

He exits.

Richard looks to the TV, then looks to Gloria sitting across the room in the chair.

RICHARD

Wanna come up here on the bed and watch TV with me?

You can tell she doesn't want to.

He pats the empty space next to him.

Come on.

She gets out of her chair, walks across to the bed and sits next to him.

EXT. PHONE BOOTH – DAY

A phone booth outside a gas station. Seth is in the middle of a conversation with the party on the other end. Seth speaks Spanish and his dialogue is subtitled into English beneath him.

SETH

Things are real hot here. Crossing's gonna be a bitch.
(*pause*)
Don't worry, we'll get across. But when we do, where do we go?
(*pause*)
Can we make it as close to the border as possible? Texas wants our balls. The quicker we're in your protection, the better I'll feel.
(*pause*)
Okay, where?
(*pause; in English*)
The Titty Twister?
(*laughs*)
I love it already. Okay, Carlos, I'll see you and your men at the (*in English*) Titty Twister tomorrow morning.
(*pause*)
Bye, my friend.

Seth hangs up the phone, lights up a cigarette with his Zippo lighter and exits frame. After Seth exits, leaving the frame empty, a subtitle appears:

CUT TO:

INT. SETH'S AND RICHARD'S MOTEL ROOM – NIGHT

Richard lies on the bed by himself, propped up by pillows, watching TV, taking hits from a bong in the shape of a wizard.

On TV, a local newscaster named Kelly Houge is reporting a story about the brothers.

KELLY HOUGE
(*to camera*)

This bloody crime spree started just a week ago today. The oldest of the two brothers . . .

Mug shot of Seth.

(*voice-over*)

. . . Seth Gecko was serving time in Rolling's Kansas State Penitentiary for his part in the 1988 Scott City bank robbery in which two law enforcement officers lost their lives.

Back to: Kelly.

Having served eight years of his twenty-two-year sentence, Seth Gecko was brought to Wichita Municipal Court-house for his parole hearing. It was while at the Court-house that this man . . .

Mug shot of Richard.

(*voice-over*)

. . . his younger brother Richard Gecko, a known armed robber and sex offender, pulled off a daring daylight escape.

Back to: Kelly.

Resulting in the death of four Wichita law enforcement officers, and this woman . . .

Photo of woman smiling.

(voice-over)

. . . Heidi Vogel, sixth-grade teacher, who was run over by the Geckos during a high-speed pursuit through downtown Wichita.

On map of America.

A red line travels from Wichita to Oklahoma.

(voice-over)

From there the brothers traveled from Kansas through Oklahoma . . .

The red line enters Texas and the camera moves into Texas.

. . . into the great state of Texas. And then finally . . .

We zoom in on Abilene, circled in red.

. . . into Abilene.

We hear gunfire and screams.

CUT TO:

EXT. THE CRIMINAL COURT BUILDING – DAY

Kelly Houge walks down the court-house steps of the criminal courts building of Abilene. She talks to the camera. Cops, lawyers and citizens bustle in the background.

KELLY HOUGE

The list of the dead climbed up three more notches since our last telecast.

CUT TO:

Photo: Officer Sherman Goodell in full police uniform.

(voice-over)

Officer Sherman Goodell, who was in intensive care following the gun battle outside of the Valley Federal Bank building . . .

CUT TO:

EXT. COURT-HOUSE – DAY

Kelly Houge standing on the court-house steps talking into the camera.

. . . died about forty-five minutes ago at Hopkins General Hospital. And about six hours ago, during a daylight liquor store robbery in Big Springs, the Gecko brothers killed another Texas Ranger . . .

CUT TO:

Photo: Earl McGraw in uniform.

(voice-over)

. . . Earl McGraw.

CUT TO:

Photo: Pete in a Hawaiian shirt holding up a big fish.

. . . and liquor store clerk Pete Bottoms.

CUT TO:

Video footage: Benny's World of Liquor burning down.

Then they proceeded to burn the store down to the ground.

CUT TO:

Video graphic: Picture of the Gecko brothers with a tally underneath:

THE GECKO BROTHERS
WICHITA JAIL BREAK
VALLEY FEDERAL BANK ROBBERY
BIG SPRINGS CONVENIENCE STORE ROBBERY

DEATH TOLL
13

TEXAS RANGERS	POLICE OFFICERS	CIVILIANS
4	7	2

That changes the death toll to fifteen.

(figure changes under 'death toll')

Five Texas Rangers . . .

(figure changes)

Eight police officers . . .

(figure changes)

Three civilians.

(figure changes)

CUT TO:

Back to: Kelly.
And one hostage . . .
CUT TO:

Photo: Gloria Hill.

(voice-over)

. . . bank teller and mother of four, Gloria Hill.

Kelly to camera.

Heading the case to bring these fugitives to justice is FBI Agent
Stanley Chase. We talked with Agent Chase earlier this afternoon.
CUT TO:

VIDEO INTERVIEW

Kelly Houge interviewing Stanley Chase of the FBI.

STANLEY CHASE

For the time being we are very confident we will apprehend the
fugitives in the next forty-eight hours. The Bureau, local law
enforcement and the Texas Rangers have all joined forces in
forming a dragnet to snare Seth and Richard Gecko.

KELLY HOUGE

Agent Chase, does it appear that they are heading for Mexico?

STANLEY CHASE

Yes, it does, Kelly. We have already alerted the Mexican
authorities. They intend to cooperate in every way possible to
bring these fugitives to justice.

KELLY HOUGE

Are you optimistic about the safety of the hostage they took in
Abilene, Gloria Hill?

STANLEY CHASE

We've received no news one way or the other. We can only hope
for the best.

KELLY HOUGE

What about the report from an eyewitness at the liquor store who
said one of the brothers was shot?

26

STANLEY CHASE

This can't be confirmed at this time, but we do believe it to be true. We have reason to believe it was the younger brother, Richard, and he was shot in the vicinity of his neck and shoulders by the store's clerk.

KELLY HOUGE

Is it safe to assume that because the death count involved the loss of life of law enforcement officers, that the Bureau, the Rangers and the police force are taking this manhunt personally?

STANLEY CHASE

I would say that's a very safe assumption.

CUT TO:

Richard smiles.

RICHARD
(*Newscaster's voice*)

Is it safe to assume since the law enforcement authorities in the great state of Texas are homosexuals of a sick and deviate nature, that they will be too busy fucking each other up the ass to actually catch the Gecko brothers?

(*FBI voice*)

I would say that's a very safe assumption.

He changes channel on the TV. We see a Casper the Friendly Ghost *cartoon on the screen.*

CASPER

Would you play with me?

A big burly Cop turns around.

COP

Sure, little boy . . . A ghost !!!

The cop heads for the hills. Casper cries.

Seth enters the room carrying a six-pack of beer and two take-out bags of Big Kahuna burgers.

RICHARD

Shit, I started to get worried. Where the fuck ya been?

SETH

Sightseein'.

RICHARD

What'd ya see?

SETH

Cops.

RICHARD

Did ya look at the border?

Seth dumps the burgers on the bed. Both men pop beers and Richard goes to town on a hamburger. Seth flips off the TV.

SETH

Yeah, I saw the border. Through binoculars from on top of a high building. That's about as close as I risked getting. What's the TV say?

RICHARD

They're going to apprehend us in forty-eight hours.

Seth sits down and takes a hit of his beer.

SETH
(*to himself*)

I gotta figure a way to get across that goddamn border. Longer we fuck around El Paso, our lives ain't worth a shit.

RICHARD

Look, fuck the border. Let's just dig in and wait for things to cool down.

SETH

Richie, it's gonna get a lot fuckin' worse before it gets any fuckin' better. We showed our ass in Texas. We killed Texas police officers. We killed Texas fuckin' Rangers. They ain't gonna stop lookin' till they find us, and when they find us, they're gonna kill us. Texans take it very personal when ya kill their law enforcement officers. The El Paso police have already started a motel and hotel search for us.

RICHARD

How do you know?

SETH

I heard it on the radio. We gotta get our asses into Mexico tonight. Carlos is gonna meet us tomorrow morning at a rendezvous on the other side, then Carlos and his boys will escort us to El Ray and –

Seth stops talking and looks around.

Where's the woman?

RICHARD

What?

Seth's out of his chair.

SETH

What'd ya mean, what? The fuckin' woman, the hostage. Where the fuck is she, Richard!?

RICHARD

She's in the other room.

SETH

What the fuck is she doin' there?!

He goes to the door of the adjoining room.

RICHARD

Seth, before you open the door, let me explain what happened.

Seth stops and looks at his brother. He knows what he means. He can't say anything, only point at his younger sibling. Then he bursts open the door.

The dead, naked body of Gloria Hill lies on the bed. It's obvious Richard raped and killed her.

Seth covers his eyes with his hands. He slowly enters the room with the dead body.

SETH
(*to himself*)

Oh, Richard, what's wrong with you?

Richard rises from the bed.

RICHARD

Now, Seth, before you flip out, let me just explain what happened.

Seth slowly turns to his brother, then walks toward him.

Richard backs up.

SETH

Yeah, explain it to me. I need an explanation. What's the matter with you?

RICHARD
(*low and calm*)

There's nothing wrong with me, brother. That woman tried to escape and I did what I had to do.

SETH

No.
(*pause*)

That woman wouldn't've said shit if she had a mouthful.

RICHARD

Wrong, wrong, wrong, wrong, wrong, wrong, wrong! Once you left, she became a whole different person.

SETH
(*slowly approaching*)

Is it me? Is it my fault?

RICHARD

It's not your fault, it's her fault!

Seth grabs Richard and throws him in the corner of the room, holding tightly to his wrist.

SETH

Is this my fault? Do you think this is what I am?

RICHARD

What?

SETH

This is not me! I am a professional fucking thief. I steal money.

31

You try to stop me, God help you. But I don't kill people I don't have to, and I don't rape women. What you doin' ain't how it's done. Do you understand?

RICHARD

Seth, if you were me –

SETH

Just say yes! Nothing else, just say yes.

RICHARD

Yes.

SETH

Yes, Seth, I understand.

RICHARD

Yes, Seth, I understand.

Seth hugs his little brother. Tight.

SETH
(*whispers in Richard's ear*)

We get into Mexico, it's gonna be sweet Rosemary, hundred-proof liquor, and rice and beans. None of this shit's gonna matter.

INT. MOTOR HOME – NIGHT

Scott and Kate are in the front seat of their parked motor home. The motor home's parked in front of the Dew Drop Inn's front office. We see Jacob inside, getting a room from the Old-Timer.

KATE

I can't believe he's stopping here. This place looks totally cruddy.

Jacob walks out of the office. Kate yells from the motor home.

Dad, why are we stopping here?

He opens the motor home door and climbs in.

JACOB

There's nothing wrong with this place.

KATE

It's a flop house.

JACOB

It's not a flop house. It's basic and simple. That doesn't make it a flop house.

KATE

If it doesn't have a pool, we're looking for a new place.

Starting the huge car and slowly maneuvering it through the courtyard.

JACOB

It has a bed. That's all I care about.

KATE

Other places have beds, they also have cable TV, a gym, room service . . .

EXT. COURTYARD – NIGHT

Seth walks out of Room 9 with a beer in his hand. He's thinking about how he's going to get over the border tonight. Lost in thought, he steps out in the path of the Fullers' motor home.

Jacob slams on the brakes.

Seth jumps back, startled.

Both Kate and Scott are tossed out of their seats on to the floor. Thud . . . Thud . . .

KATE

Owww, my head.

Jacob, pissed, honks his horn at Seth and yells out the window.

JACOB

Watch where you're going!

Through windshield: Seth just stands right in their way without moving, gazing up at the giant motor home.

Jacob behind the wheel: Kate and Scott join him up front looking at this weirdo.

SCOTT

What's this guy's problem?

33

I have no idea.

Seth continues standing in their way, making no attempt to move. Not threatening, just looking at them.

HONK!

Any time, man.

The horn snaps Seth back to this world. A smile breaks out on the escaped fugitive's face and he politely steps to one side to let them pass.

Pass they do!

KATE

Creepy guy.

On Seth: the Sword of Damocles is lifted from over his head. He's just solved a problem that a mere thirty seconds ago seemed unsolvable. He knows exactly how he's going to cross the border. Whistling a happy tune, he turns and walks back into Room 9.

INT. FULLERS' MOTEL ROOM – NIGHT

The Fullers are in Room 12. It's identical to the one that the Gecko boys are in, except that the paintings above the beds are different. Jacob has fallen asleep in his clothes on the bed.

Scott sits in a chair, headphones on, playing an unplugged electric guitar. Kate is nowhere in sight.

Knock . . . knock . . . knock . . . on the door.

Scott doesn't hear shit but his music.

Jacob stirs a bit, but doesn't wake up.

Pound . . . pound . . . pound . . . on the door.

Jacob springs up. He looks over at Scott, who, lost in guitar heaven, is oblivious of the knocker, then to the door.

JACOB
(*yelling*)

What?

From the other side of the door comes a friendly voice.

VOICE
(*off-screen*)

I'm your neighbour in Room 9. I hate to disturb you, but I'd like
to ask a favor.

*Jacob swings his feet to the floor, stands up and walks to the door. As
he passes Scott, he says, in his direction –*

JACOB

I hope none of this is disturbing you.

*Scott can't hear him, but when he sees his Dad look at him, he
smiles.*

Jacob opens the door and sees . . .

*. . . Richard Gecko standing in the doorway, looking like the nicest
guy in the entire world.*

RICHARD

Hi there, I'm from Room 9, my name is Don Cornelius. No, not
the Don Cornelius from *Soul Train*. Me and my lady friend need
some ice and we don't seem to have an ice bucket. Could we
possibly borrow yours? I'll bring it right back.

JACOB
(*still partially asleep*)

Sure.

*We follow Jacob as he turns to the dresser to get the motel ice bucket.
He grabs it, turns back to the door, takes a couple of steps towards it,
then stops in his tracks.*

*He sees Richard and Seth both inside the room with the door closed,
both with .45s in their hands, both aimed at him.*

What is this?

Seth slugs Jacob in the mouth, knocking him to the ground.

35

SETH

It's called a punch.

Scott suddenly becomes aware of what's going on around him and instinctively stands. Richard shoves his .45 in Scott's mouth.

RICHARD

Sit down.

Scott lowers himself back down on to his seat.

Good boy.

Jacob lifts his head off the floor and wipes blood away from his lip. He looks at his opponent who stands over him.

SETH
(to Jacob)

What's your name?

JACOB

Jacob.

SETH

Okay, Jacob, get up and sit your ass down on the bed. Make a wrong move and I'll shoot you in the face.

Jacob rises and sits on the edge of the bed.

(to Richard)

Okay, move the Jap over there.

Keeping the gun in Scott's mouth, Richard makes Scott rise . . .

RICHARD

Upsy daisy.

. . . guiding him over to the bed by his father.

Richard removes the gun from Scott's mouth and stands next to his brother, looking down at their two hostages.

SETH
(to his hostages)

What's the story with you two? You a couple of fags?

JACOB

He's my son.

SETH

How does that happen? You don't look Japanese.

JACOB

Neither does he. He looks Vietnamese.

SETH

Oh, well, excuse me all to hell.

JACOB

What's this about, money?

SETH

It's about money, all right, but not yours. You see, me and my brother here are in a little hot water and we need your assistance.

The door to Room 12 opens and a dripping-wet, bikini-clad Kate walks in.

The brothers spin their guns in her direction.

Kate, startled, screams.

Jacob and Scott get on their feet and move forward.

Seth spins back towards the two men, gun ready to spit.

(*to Scott and Jacob*)

Stop!

Jacob and Scott freeze.

Richard moves like quicksilver, shutting the door and positioning himself behind the terrified Kate.

KATE

What's going on?

RICHARD

We're having a wet bikini contest, and you just won.

(*to Kate*)

It's okay, honey. Everything's going to be all right.

SETH

Just listen to Daddy, sugar, and don't do nothin' stupid.

He turns to Jacob and Scott who are still standing.

You two, Simon says sit the fuck down!

They slowly sit.

Richard can't take his eyes off the dripping-wet Kate.

Both Jacob and Seth see this and neither men like it. Both for their own reasons.

(*to Jacob*)

Where are the keys to the motor home?

JACOB

On the dresser.

SETH

Richie, take the keys. Start that big bastard up, and drive it up front.

Richard doesn't move from his position behind Kate.

Kate feels his eyes on her.

She slowly turns and looks at him.

He looks in her face.

Close-up: Kate. She smiles at him.

KATE

Richie, will you do me a favor and eat my pussy?

Close-up: Richard.

RICHARD

Sure.

(off-screen)

Richard!

Richard's eyes go to Seth.

Everybody is where they were. Kate never turned around.

SETH

Not when you get around to it. Now.

Without saying a word, he takes the keys and leaves the room.

(pointing at Kate)

You, Gidget, go in the bathroom and put on some clothes.

She grabs some clothes from the floor and moves towards the bathroom.

Seth grabs her wrist.

You got three minutes. One second longer, I shoot your father in the face. Do you understand what I just said?

KATE

Yes.

SETH

Do you believe me?

KATE

Yes.

SETH

You damn well better. Go.

She goes into the bathroom.

JACOB

Look, if you want the motor home, just take it and get out.

Seth grabs a chair and slides it up to his two male hostages.

SETH

Sorry, Pops, it ain't gonna be that easy.

We hear the motor home honk twice outside.

Get ready to move out, we're all going on a little ride.

Jacob shakes his head 'no'.

JACOB

Not a chance.

SETH

Come again?

JACOB

If you're taking people, take me. But my kids aren't going anywhere with you.

SETH

Sorry, I need everybody.

JACOB

My children are not going with you, and that's that.

SETH
(*angry*)

That's not fuckin' that . . .

He holds up his gun.

. . . this is fuckin' this.

He calms down and looks at Scott.

Go sit over there.

Scott gets up and walks to the other side of the room, leaving the two men alone. Seth speaks in a quiet, conversational tone.

I ain't got time to fuck around with you, so I'll make this simple. Take your kids and get in the car, or I'll execute all three of you right now.

He cocks the gun and puts it right in Jacob's face.

What's it gonna be, yes or no answer?

Jacob looks at him.

JACOB

Yes.

Good.

> (*to Scott*)

Your old man's all right, he just saved your life.

Seth bangs on the bathroom door.

Time's up, Princess.

The bathroom door opens. Kate stands there, wearing a Bullwinkle T-shirt, jeans and bare feet.

Okay, ramblers, let's get to rambling.

CUT TO:

EXT. HIGHWAY – NIGHT

The motor home with the powder keg interior drives through the Lone Star night.

INT. MOTOR HOME – NIGHT

Richard's in the back bed area with a gun trained on Kate and Scott. The two scared siblings hold hands.

KATE

Excuse me.

Richard zeros in on her.

RICHARD

What?

KATE

Where are you taking us?

RICHARD

Mexico.

KATE

What's in Mexico?

RICHARD

Mexicans.

He doesn't smile.

In the front part of the motor home, Jacob sits behind the wheel, driving into the night. Seth sits in the passenger seat, going through Jacob's wallet and talking to him calmly.

SETH
(*reading Jacob's driver's license*)
Jacob Fuller. Jacob, that's biblical, ain't it? What am I askin' for? Of course it is.
(*motioning behind him*)
What are their names?

JACOB
Scott and Kate.

Seth repeats the names as he thumbs through the wallet.

SETH
Scott and Kate . . . Kate and Scott . . . Scott Fuller . . . Kate Fuller . . .

Seth looks back at the wallet. He sees Jacob's minister's license.

Is this real?

JACOB
Yes.

SETH
I've seen one of these before. A friend of mine had himself declared a minister of his own religion. A way to fuck the IRS. Is that what you're doing, or are you the real McCoy?

JACOB
Real McCoy.

SETH
You're a preacher?

JACOB
I was a minister.

SETH
Was? As in not any more?

43

JACOB

Yes.

SETH

Why'd ya quit?

JACOB

I think I've gotten about as up close and personal with you as I'm gonna get. Now if you need me like I think you need me, you're not gonna kill me 'cause I won't answer your stupid, prying questions. So, with all due respect, mind your own business.

SETH

I seem to have touched a nerve. Don't be so sensitive, Pops, let's keep this friendly. But you're right, enough with the getting to know you shit. Now, there's two ways we can play this hand.

Seth comes to a snapshot of Jacob and his wife.

Who's this?

JACOB

My wife.

SETH

Where is the little lady?

JACOB

In heaven.

SETH

She's dead?

JACOB

Yes, she is.

SETH

How'd she die?

JACOB

Auto wreck.

SETH

Come on, gimme some more details. How'd it happen? Some fuckin' drunk kill her?

44

JACOB

No. It was a rainy night, the brakes on the car weren't great. She had to stop suddenly. She slid on the road, she crashed, she died.

SETH

Died instantly?

JACOB

Not quite. She was trapped in the wreck for about six hours before she passed on.

SETH

Whewww! Those acts of God really stick it in and break it off, don't they?

JACOB

Yes they do.

SETH

One way is me and you go round an' round all fuckin' night. The other way, is we reach some sort of an understanding. Now, if we go down that first path at the end of the day, I'll win. But if we go down the second, we'll both win. Now, I don't give a rat's ass about you or your fuckin' family. Y'all can live forever or die this second and I don't care which. The only things I do care about are *me*, that son-of-a-bitch in the back and our money. And right now I need to get those three things into Mexico. Now, stop me if I'm wrong, but I take it you don't give a shit about seeing me and my brother receiving justice, or the bank getting its money back. Right now all you care about is the safety of your daughter, your son and possibly yourself. Am I correct?

JACOB

Yes.

SETH

I thought so. You help us get across the border without incident, stay with us the rest of the night without trying anything funny, and in the morning we'll let you and your family go. That way everybody gets what they want. You and your kids get out of this alive and we get into Mexico. Everybody's happy.

JACOB

How do I know you'll keep your word?

SETH

Jesus Christ, Pops, don't start with this shit.

JACOB

You want me to sit here and be passive. The only way being
passive in this situation makes sense is if I believe you'll let us go.
I'm not there yet. You have to convince me you're telling the
truth.

SETH

Look, dickhead, the only thing you need to be convinced about is
that you're stuck in a situation with a coupla real mean
motorscooters. I don't wanna hafta worry about you all fuckin'
night. And I don't think you wanna be worrying about my
brother's intentions toward your daughter all night. You notice
the way he looked at her, didn't ya?

JACOB

Yes.

SETH

Didn't like it, did ya?

JACOB

No, I didn't.

SETH

Didn't think so. So, as I was saying, I'm willing to make a deal.
You behave, get us into Mexico, and don't try to escape. I'll keep
my brother off your daughter and let you all loose in the morning.

JACOB

You won't let him touch her?

SETH

I can handle Richie, don't worry.

The two men look at each other for some measure of trust.

Seth sticks out his hand.

I give you my word.

Seth can't help but think about the last time he gave his word.

> (*hand sticks out*)

My word's my law. Better you not take it, and that's just where we are, than take it and not mean it.

Jacob takes his hand, but looks right into Seth.

JACOB

If he touches her, I'll kill him. I don't give a fuck how many guns you have, nothing will stop me from killing him.

SETH

Fair enough. You break your word, I'll kill all of you.

> (*calling to the back*)

Kate, honey!

KATE

Yeah.

SETH

You must have a bible in here, don'tcha?

KATE

Yeah, we got a bible.

SETH

Get it and bring it up here, will ya, please?

Kate goes into a drawer, pulls out a bible and brings it up front.

Hold it right there, sweetie pie.

> (*to Jacob*)

Put your hand on it.

Jacob does.

Swear to God, on the Bible, you won't try to escape and you'll get us across the border.

JACOB

I swear to God I won't try to escape and I'll do my best to get you into Mexico.

SETH

You best better get it done, Pops.

Seth places his hand on the Bible.

I swear to God I'll let you loose in the morning. And your daughter will be safe. And I also swear if you do anything to fuck me up, I'll slit all your throats.

TIME CUT TO:

INT. MOTOR HOME – NIGHT

Richard's in the back with Kate and Scott. Richard, expressionless, looks at Kate's bare feet.

Slow zoom Kate's bare feet.

Extreme close-up: Kate's toes. They wiggle.

His eyes go to her hands.

Slow zoom Kate's hands.

Extreme close-up: Kate's fingers.

His eyes go to her neck.

Slow zoom nape of Kate's neck.

Extreme close-up: Kate's Adam's apple. She swallows.

His eyes move up.

Side profile of Kate, slow zoom to Kate's lips.

Back to: Richard.

RICHARD
Didya mean what you said back there?

Kate turns to him.

KATE
What?

RICHARD
In the room. Were you serious, or were you just foolin' around? I'm just bringing it up, 'cause if you really want me to do that for you I will.

48

                              KATE
Do what?

                             RICHARD
                          (*in a whisper*)
What you said to me in the room.

                              KATE
                         (*whispers back*)
What did I say?

                             RICHARD
                            (*whispers*)
You asked me if I would –

                              SETH
                          (*off-screen*)
Richard!

                             RICHARD
                            (*to Seth*)
What?

Seth and Jacob.

                              SETH
I told you to watch those kids, I didn't say talk to 'em. You guys
ain't got nothin' to say to one another. So cut the chatter.

Richard turns to Kate.

                             RICHARD
                            (*quiet*)
We'll talk later.

Kate still hasn't a clue what he means.
CUT TO:

EXT. THE MEXICAN BORDER – NIGHT

*Automobiles are lined up, waiting one by one to go into Mexico. Cop
cars with their red and blue lights flashing are all over the place. Border
patrol men and police are stopping all cars. Pulling up to the end of the
line is the Fullers' mobile home.*

INT. MOTOR HOME – NIGHT

Jacob at the wheel, Seth in the passenger seat. Seth jumps up and goes into action.

> SETH

Okay everybody, it's show time. Richie, take Kate in the bathroom.

> *Richard grabs the terrified Kate and drags her in the bathroom.*

Scott, you come up front with your daddy.

> *Scott does. Seth, keeping low, gets behind Jacob.*

> JACOB

I'm telling you, don't hurt her.

> SETH

As long as you're cool, she'll be cool. What're ya gonna say?

> JACOB

I don't have the slightest idea.

> SETH

Well, you just keep thinkin' of that gun next to Kate's temple.

> *Seth disappears into the bathroom with Kate and Richard, closing the door behind him.*

> *Father and son are alone for the first time since this whole thing began.*

> SCOTT

What are you gonna do?

> JACOB

I'm gonna try and get us across the border.

> SCOTT

No, Dad, you gotta tell 'em that they're back there.

> *Jacob is surprised to hear Scott say this.*

INT. BATHROOM – MOTOR HOME – NIGHT

The bathroom, which consists of a shower, a toilet and a small sink, is a tight fit with three people in it.

Richard has his neck against the wall, with his arm around Kate, holding her in front of him. One hand is over her mouth, the other holds a .45 against her head.

Kate's eyes are wide with fear.

Seth stands, .45 in hand, ready to fire if the wrong person should open the door.

Everybody talks low and quiet.

> RICHARD

This isn't gonna work.

> SETH

Shut up. It's gonna work just fine.

> RICHARD

I just want to go on record as saying this is a bad idea.

> SETH

Duly noted. Now, shut up.

Everyone's quiet for a second, till Richard breaks it.

> RICHARD
> (*to himself*)

They're gonna search the van.

> SETH
> (*off-hand*)

As long as you don't act like a fuckin' nut, we'll be just fine.

> RICHARD

What does that mean?

> SETH
> (*distracted*)

What?

Richard lets Kate go, she quickly moves to the side.

RICHARD

You just called me a fuckin' nut.

SETH

No, I didn't.

RICHARD

Yes, you did. You said as long as I don't act like a fuckin' nut, implying that I've been acting like a fuckin' nut.

SETH

Take a pill, kid. I just meant stay cool.

RICHARD

You meant that, but you meant the other, too.

Kate can't believe what she's watching.

Neither can Seth.

SETH
(*serious as a heart attack*)

This ain't the time, Richard.

RICHARD
(*his voice rising*)

Fuck, those spic pigs! You called me a fuckin' nut, and where I come from, that stops the train on its tracks.

SETH
(*real quiet and violent*)

Keep your voice down.

RICHARD
(*quiet back*)

Or what?

BACK TO:

FRONT SEAT OF MOTOR HOME

JACOB

Have you forgotten about your sister?

SCOTT

They're gonna kill us. They get us across the border, they're gonna take us out in the desert and shoot us.

JACOB

If they get over the border, they're gonna let us go.

SCOTT

Dad, I watch those reality shows. They never let anybody go. Any cop will tell you, in a situation like this, you get a chance, you go for it. This is our chance.

JACOB

What about Kate?

SCOTT

Richie is gonna rape and kill Kate before the night's over. At least now with all these cops she's got a fighting chance.

JACOB

Seth wouldn't let him do that. He gave me his word.

SCOTT

Oh, why didn't you say that? I feel so much better. Seth's a killer, a thief, and a kidnapper, but I'm sure he's not a liar.

JACOB

Son, it may not seem like it, but I know exactly what I'm doing. You're going to have to trust me on this.

SCOTT

If trusting you means trusting those fuckin' killers, I can't do that. If you don't tell the cops, I will.

Jacob grabs Scott by the front of his shirt, and yanks him to him.

JACOB

Now, you listen to me. You ain't gonna do a goddamn fucking thing, you hear me! Nobody cares what you think, I'm running this show, I make the decisions.

SCOTT

He's running the show.

JACOB

I'm running the show. I make the plays, and you back the plays I make. Stop thinking with your fucking balls. Kate in a room with a couple of desperate men with nothing to fucking lose ain't the time to 'go for it'. I need your cover. Cover my ass.

There's a honk behind them.

They both look out the window.

It's their turn with the border patrol guards.

Jacob takes the wheel and drives up.

A stern Border Guard approaches Jacob's window.

BORDER GUARD

How many with you?

JACOB

Just my son and I.

BORDER GUARD

What is your purpose in Mexico?

JACOB

Vacation. I'm taking him to see his first bullfight.

BACK TO:

BATHROOM

RICHARD

I'm curious. What was the nuttiest thing I did?

SETH

This ain't the time.

RICHARD

Oh, I know, was it possibly when your ass was rotting in jail and I broke it out? Yeah, you're right, that was pretty fuckin' nutty. Not to mention stupid. But you know what? I can fix that right now.

Seth hauls off and punches Richard smack in the head.

Richard hits the floor.

54

GUARD AND JACOB

Guard, Jacob, and Scott hear Richard fall in the bathroom.

BORDER GUARD

What was that?

JACOB

Oh, that's just my daughter in the bathroom.

BORDER GUARD

You said it was just you and your son.

JACOB

I meant me, my son and my daughter.

Close-up: Border Guard.

BORDER GUARD

Open the door. I'm coming aboard.

BACK TO:

BATHROOM

Close-up: Kate.

We can only see Kate's face. It's scared. We hear rustling around the bathroom, but we don't know what it is.

Then it's quiet. Then we hear talking outside the door, but we can't make it out. Then we hear a knock.

KATE

I'm in the bathroom.

BORDER GUARD
(*off-screen*)

It's the Border Patrol. Open up.

KATE

It's open.

We hear the door open and see the light change on Kate's face. She's looking up.

Border Guard in the doorway looking in.

He sees: Kate by herself, pants around her ankles, sitting on the toilet.

                              KATE
Do you mind? Shut the fucking door.

                        BORDER GUARD
Excuse me.

He closes the door.

Kate lets out a breath.

We wait a beat, Seth pulls back the curtain in the shower, we see Richie on the floor of the shower knocked out.

Seth and Kate meet eyes.

He gives her the okay signal.
CUT TO:

BACK WINDOW OF MOTOR HOME

We see through the back window of the motor home, the border getting smaller as we move away from it.

Scott knocks on the bathroom door.

                             SCOTT
It's clear.

Seth bursts out of the bathroom.

                              SETH
Goddamn, that was intense!

Seth goes to the back window. He sees the border getting farther and farther away. No cars following.

                         (*to himself*)
We did it.
                           (*pause*)
We're in Mexico.

Seth throws his head back and screams for joy.

                               56

Kate, emerging from the bathroom, reacts to Seth's scream, along with Scott.

Seth is so happy that he does a little jig in the back of the van.

Everybody else is still tense as shit. But Seth lets go of all his tension, and becomes a new man before our eyes. He turns to Kate.

(*loud and happy*)
Come here, Kate!

Kate, nervous, takes a step back.

He charges for her. Grabs her, hugs her around her waist, and spins her around. When he lets her go, she stumbles dizzily onto the bed.

(*to Kate*)
You were magnificent! You told him to shut the fucking door. I'm hiding in the shower, and I'm thinking to myself, 'Did I just fuckin', hear what I just fuckin' heard?' And what does he do – he shuts the fucking door!

Kate kind of half smiles.

If I was a bit younger, baby, I'd fuckin' marry you!

Seth goes up front and slaps Jacob on the back.

I gotta hand it to ya, Pops, you raised a *fuckin' woman.*

Jacob doesn't share Seth's enthusiasm, but he is relieved.

JACOB
We did our part, we gotcha into Mexico. Now it's time for your part, letting us go.

SETH
Pops, when you're right, you're right, and you are right.

KATE
(*suddenly brightens*)
You're gonna let us go?

SETH
In the morning, darlin', in the morning, we are G-O-N-E and you are F-R-E-E. Now, I know I put you guys through hell, and I

57

know I've been one rough pecker, but from here on end, you guys are in my cool book. Scotty, help me pick Richie up, and lay him down. Jacob, keep going on this road till you get to a sign that says 'Digayo'. When you get to Digayo, turn this big bastard left, go down for a few miles, then you see a bar called The Titty Twister. From what I hear, you can't miss it.

JACOB

Then?

SETH

Then stop, 'cause that's where we're going.

He slaps him once again on the back, and leaves to attend to Richard.
CUT TO:

Close-up: Richard without glasses, unconscious. Seth slaps his face.

(off-screen)

C'mon, kid, wake up. Don't make a career out of it.

Richard starts coming to and opens his eyes.

Seth sits at the foot of the bed.

You okay?

RICHARD
(disoriented)

Yeah, I think so. What happened?

SETH

I don't know, you just passed out.

RICHARD

I did?

SETH

Yeah, we were just standing there. You said something about your shoulder hurting, then you just hit the ground like a sack of potatoes.

RICHARD

Really?

58

SETH

Yeah, when you fell your head smacked the toilet hard. It scared the shit outta me. Sure you're okay?

RICHARD

Yeah, I guess. I'm just a little fucked up.

SETH

Well, let me tell ya something, gonna clear your head right up. We are officially Mexicans.

RICHARD

What?

SETH

We are . . .
(*singing*)
. . . South of the border down Mexico way.

RICHARD

We are?

SETH

Yep. We're heading for the rendezvous right now. We get there, we pound booze till Carlos shows up, he escorts us to El Ray. And then me and you, brother, kick fuckin' back. How ya like them apples?

Slowly shaking the cobwebs out of his head.

RICHARD

Far out.
(*pause*)
Where are my glasses?

SETH

They broke when you fell.

RICHARD

Oh, fuck, Seth, that's my only pair!

SETH

Don't worry about it, we'll get you some glasses.

RICHARD

Whatdya mean, don't worry about it. Of course I'm gonna worry about it, I can't fuckin' see.

SETH

When we get to El Ray, I'll take care of it.

RICHARD

Yeah, like a Mexican hole-in-the-wall's gonna have my fuckin' prescription.

SETH

It's not a big deal, unless you make it a big deal. Now, I'm real happy, Richie, stop bringing me down with bullshit.

Jacob calls to the back.

JACOB

Guys! We're here.

CUT TO:

A neon sign that flashes:

THE TITTY TWISTER
BIKER/TRUCKER BAR, DUSK TILL DAWN

Underneath the joint's proud name on the sign, and on top of 'Biker/ Trucker Bar, Dusk Till Dawn' is a well-endowed woman, whose breast is being twisted by a neon hand.

EXT. TITTY TWISTER – NIGHT

The neon sign sits on top of the rudest, sleaziest, most crab-infested, strip joint, honky-tonk whorehouse in all of Mexico.

The Titty Twister is located in the middle of Nowheresville. It sits by itself with nothing around it for miles. A plethora of choppers and eighteen-wheelers are parked out in front. The walls almost pulsate from the loud, raunchy music within the structure. Signs cover the walls outside reading things like: 'NUDE DANCING', 'WHORES', 'BEER', 'AUTHENTIC MEXICAN FOOD,' 'BIKERS AND TRUCKERS ONLY', 'OPEN DUSK TILL DAWN', 'THURSDAY COCKFIGHT NIGHT', 'WEDNESDAY DOGFIGHT NIGHT', 'DONKEY SHOW MONDAYS', 'EVERY FRIDAY BARE KNUCKLE FIGHT TO THE DEATH,

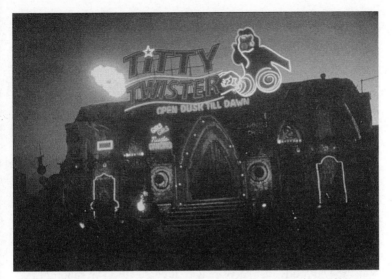

*FEATURING THE LOVELY SANTANICO PANDEMONIUM',
'ATHENA AND DANNY THE WONDER PONY' and 'THE
SLEAZY TITTY TWISTER DANCERS'.*

*In the parking lot, a biker and a truck driver beat the shit out of each
other, one with a pipe, the other with a hammer. A second biker fucks a
Titty Twister whore against the wall. A greasy man, known as Chet
Pussy, stands in the parking lot, soliciting customers through a Mr
Microphone.*

CHET

Pussy, pussy, pussy! All pussy must go. At the Titty Twister we're
slashing pussy in half! This is a pussy blow out! Make us an offer
on our vast selection of pussy! We got white pussy, black pussy,
Spanish pussy, yellow pussy, hot pussy, cold pussy, wet pussy,
tight pussy, big pussy, bloody pussy, fat pussy, hairy pussy, smelly
pussy, velvet pussy, silk pussy, Naugahyde pussy, snappin' pussy,
horse pussy, dog pussy, mule pussy, fake pussy! If we don't have
it, you don't want it!

The Fullers' recreational vehicle pulls into the parking lot and stops.

INT. MOTOR HOME – NIGHT

What's left of the Fuller family and the Gecko family look out the windshield on to the sight that is the Titty Twister.

> **SETH**
> (*to the group*)
> Okay, troops, this is the home stretch. Here's the deal; this place closes at dawn. Carlos is gonna meet us here sometime before dawn. Which by my guesstimate is somewhere between three or four hours from now. So we're gonna go in there, take a seat, have a drink – have a bunch of drinks, and wait for Carlos. That could be an hour, that could be three hours, I don't know which. But when he gets here, me and Richie are going to leave with him. After we split, you guys are officially out of this stew pot. Let me just say I'm real happy about where we're at. We got a real nice, 'I don't fuck with you – you don't fuck with me' attitude going on. Now, if everybody just keeps playin' it cool – and I'm talking to you, too, Richie – everybody's gonna get what they want. *Comprende, amigos?*

Everybody nods and mutters in agreement.

Okay hard drinkers, let's drink hard. I'm buyin'.

EXT. PARKING LOT – NIGHT

The camper door flies open and the two brothers and the Fuller family step out into the night.

They look across the parking lot at the Titty Twister. It looks like the entrance to hell.

> **JACOB**
> Out of the stew pot and into the fire.

> **SETH**
> Shit, I been to bars make this place look like a fuckin' 4-H club.

> **RICHARD**
> I gotta say I'm with Jacob on this. I been to some fucked up places in my time, but that place is fucked up.

Seth can't believe it.

SETH
(*in a baby-talk voice*)
Awww, whatsa matter, is the little baby too afraid to go into the big scary bar?

The two brothers square off, not like strangers fighting, but like brothers. They talk real quiet but real personal.

RICHARD
That's what you think?

SETH
That's how you're lookin', Richie.

RICHARD
I'm lookin' scared?

SETH
That's what you look like.

RICHARD
You know what you look like?

SETH
No, Richie, what do I look like?

RICHARD
You're lookin' green.

That's not what Seth expected to hear.

SETH
How?

RICHARD
Where are you right now?

SETH
What do you mean?

RICHARD
Where are you?

SETH
I'm here with you.

RICHARD

No, you're not. You're sippin' margaritas in El Ray. But we're not in El Ray. We're here – getting ready to go in there. You're so pleased with yourself about getting into Mexico, you think the job's down. It ain't. Get back on the clock. That's a fuck-with-you-bar. We hang around there for a coupla hours, in all likelihood, we'll get fucked with. So get your shit together, brother.

SETH

My shit is together.

RICHARD

It don't look together.

SETH

Well, it is. Just because I'm happy doesn't mean I'm on vacation. You're just not used to seein' me happy, 'cause it's been about fifteen fuckin' years since I been happy. But my shit is together.

Richard looks at him.

RICHARD

Okay . . . I'm gonna believe you.

SETH

You better believe me.

RICHARD

Now, I don't better do nothin'. I wanna believe you. But I'm watchin' you.

SETH

You'll see somethin'.

RICHARD

What'll I see?

SETH

You'll see how it's done.

RICHARD

Well, that's what I wanna see.

SETH

That's what you will see.

RICHARD

Show me.

Seth looks at Richard a moment. Holds out his fist. Richard bumps it. Then the two brothers, followed by the Fullers, move to the bar.

Chet Pussy talks into the microphone.

CHET
(*yelling into the microphone*)
Take advantage of our penny pussy sale. Buy any piece of pussy at our regular price, you get another piece of pussy, of equal or lesser value, for a penny. Now try and beat pussy for a penny! If you can find cheaper pussy anywhere, fuck it!

Chet notices our heroes, especially young Kate.

(*in microphone, towards Kate*)
What's this? A new flavor approaching. Apple Pie Pussy.

SETH

Step aside, asshole.

Chet pokes his finger in Seth's chest.

Not so fast, Slick.

Seth grabs hold of Chet's finger, bends it backwards till it snaps in two.

Chet lets out a scream.

Seth violently brings his head forward pulverizing Chet's nose.

Chet falls to his knees in front of Seth.

Seth hooks him with a powerful fist under his chin that snaps Chet's head back, and throws him on his back.

After hitting the ground, Seth sends a savage kick straight to Chet's face, rolling him over.

Chet is out.

The whole altercation took two seconds.

Everyone, in shock, looks at Seth.

Seth looks back at Richard.

> SETH

Now, is my shit together, or is my shit together?

> RICHARD
> (*bumping fist*)

Forever together!

They head for the door. Richard stays behind for a second, and gives the fallen Chet a few, swift kicks.

INT. THE TITTY TWISTER – DAY

If the Titty Twister looked like the asshole of the world from the outside, in the immortal words of Al Jolson, 'You ain't seen nothin' yet.' This is the kind of place where they sweep up the teeth and hose down the cum, the blood and the beer at closing.

In the back, topless dancers do lap dances with customers, while a sleazy sexy stripper strips to raunchy music, played at an eardrum-bursting level. Two men are in a savage bare knuckle fight, surrounded by screaming customers of bikers and truckers.

One of the dancers is a man with a saddle on his back, his name is Danny the Wonder Pony. The woman on his back, in the saddle, feet in the stirrups, hands on the reins, is Athena, his rider. They dance around to the cheers of the crowd.

Bikers and truckers play pool in the back. Fights break out here about every ten minutes. The customers may start 'em, but the bouncer, Big Emilio, ends 'em.

Seth, Richard, Jacob, Scott and Kate walk through the door.

They each take in the sights and the smells.

Seth is the first to say something.

> SETH

Now this is my kinda place! I could become a regular.

The man behind the bar is Razor Charlie. He eyes the group as they approach.

Their dissimilarity to the usual road waif nomads who populate the Twister disturbs him. He exchanges a knowing look across the room with Big Emilio, as the group bellies up to the bar.

Whisky!

RAZOR CHARLIE
(in English)

You can't come in here.

SETH

Whatcha mean?

RAZOR CHARLIE

This is a private club. You're not welcome.

SETH

Are you tellin' me I'm not good enough to drink *here*?

RAZOR CHARLIE

This bar is for bikers and truckers only.

He points his finger to Seth.

You, get out!

Big Emilio almost magically appears behind Seth and places his big beefy sausage-fingered hand hard on Seth's shoulder.

BIG EMILIO
(to Seth, in Spanish)

Walk, Pendaho.

Seth slowly turns his eyes to the big hand on his shoulder.

SETH
(low)

Take your hand off me.

BIG EMILIO
(in Spanish)

I'm going to count to three.

No, I'm going to count to three.

BIG EMILIO

Uno . . .

SETH

Two . . .

Jacob jumps in the middle.

JACOB

Now wait a minute, there's no reason to get ugly. There's just a misunderstanding going on here. You said this bar is for truckers and bikers. Well, I'm a truck driver.

Everybody looks at Jacob.

As Jacob talks, he takes out his wallet.

If you look outside your door, parked in your parking lot, you'll see a big-ass recreational vehicle. That's mine. In order to drive that legally, you need a class two driver's license. That is the same license that the DMV requires truck drivers to carry in order to drive a truck.

He takes the license out of his wallet and lays it on the bar.

That is me, and this is my class two license. This is a truck drivers' bar, I am a truck driver, and these are my friends.

Everybody's a little stunned after Jacob's speech.

Razor Charlie picks up the license, looks at Jacob, looks at everyone in the party and smiles.

RAZOR CHARLIE
(*to Jacob*)

Welcome to the Titty Twister. What can I get you?

Seth brushes off Big Emilio's paw.

SETH

Bottle of whisky and five glasses.

Razor Charlie's eyes go to Seth. Even though he has a big smile on his face, he looks as if he's going to kill Seth. But instead he just says:

RAZOR CHARLIE

Coming right up.

Razor Charlie goes for the bottle.

Big Emilio gives the party one last look and walks away.

Richard gives Jacob a buddy punch on the shoulder.

RICHARD

Good job, Pops.

Seth's still frying an egg on his head.

SETH

That's just fuckin' typical. Biggest number one problem with Mexico, it's not service-oriented. I was feelin' so good, and those fuckin' spics brought me down.

Richard puts his arm around Seth.

RICHARD

Fuck 'em, shake it off.

Razor Charlie brings the bottle and the glasses.

Seth looks at the guy, still pissed.

SETH

You serve food, José?

Razor Charlie knows Seth's taunting him with a racial slur. But he just smiles and says,

RAZOR CHARLIE

Best in Mexico.

SETH

I kinda doubt that. We're grabbin' a table, send over a waitress to take our order.

Seth walks away, and the group follows him.

We just hang on the evil wheels turning inside of Razor Charlie's head.

70

The five of them move across the floor to a table. As they walk, Kate attracts stares, wolf whistles and rude comments from some of the patrons. Jacob keeps near his daughter.

The dancers do their sexy routines. A big-chested, wild-haired blonde catches Scott's eye. She winks at him.

RICHARD

Any time you want a lap dance with that broad, say the word. It's on me, kiddo.

He gives the boy's neck a squeeze.

Jacob's eyes survey the surroundings.

Big Emilio and Razor Charlie quietly exchange words about the party in Spanish.

RAZOR CHARLIE
(*in Spanish*)

They're not the usual road trash we normally feed on. But it'll be okay. No one knows they're here.

The five of them find a table and sit down.

Seth, still in a bad mood, takes the cork out of the whisky bottle and tosses it. He pours Richie and himself a glass.

SETH

Who else?

JACOB

Pass.

SETH
(*picking a fight*)

Why not, against your religion?

JACOB
(*won't be baited*)

No, I do drink, I'm just not drinking now.

SETH

Suit yourself, more for me.

(*to Scott*)

Scotty?

Scott shakes his head 'no'.

(*to Kate*)

How 'bout you?

KATE

I can't. I'm not twenty-one yet.

Seth smiles.

SETH

That means yes.

He pours her a drink. She looks down at it.

Seth and Richard pick up their glasses.

Post time, Kate.

Kate takes the shot glass in her hand and brings it to her lips like she's going to take a sip.

This ain't Kentucky sipping whisky. It's Mexican rot gut. You knock it down in one shot. Here we go. One . . . two . . . three.

The three of them knock back the booze. Kate's whole body does a non-drinker's tremor. Seth and Richard laugh.

That a girl.

Jacob notices something that seems strange. All the windows in the joint are plastered over.

JACOB

Did you notice this place doesn't have any windows?

SETH

It's a strip joint whorehouse. How many windows do you expect it to have?

JACOB

Look, you're at where you need to be. Why don't you let the kids go? They won't do anything while you have me.

72

SETH

Shut up. I told ya what the plan was, and what it wasn't, was open to debate. Besides, these two . . .

(*pointing at Scott and Kate*)

. . . are safer in here with us than wandering around a Mexican border town all night long. Just don't do nothin' stupid and we'll all get along fine.

(*to Scott*)

Scotty, you sure you don't want a drink?

SCOTT

Okay, I'll have one.

JACOB

No you won't.

Seth pours Scott a shot.

SETH

Sorry, Pops, but I'm drinkin' and I don't like drinkin' alone. Bottoms up, boy.

Scott takes the drink and he, too, experiences a non-drinker's tremor.

Seth turns to Kate.

How about you, cutie pie? Ready for round two?

KATE

Okay.

Seth just passes her the bottle. She pours her own shot and knocks it back.

RICHARD

(*to Seth*)

Hey, Dr Frankenstein, I think you just created a monster.

Jacob turns to Seth and asks quietly:

JACOB

Why are you so agitated?

SETH

I'm still stewing about that ape laying hands on me. And that fuckin' bartender sticks a weed up my ass, too.

JACOB

He backed down.

SETH

He's smilin' at us. But behind his smile, he's sayin', 'Fuck you, Jack.' I hear that loud and clear.

JACOB

What are you going to do?

SETH
(*picking up the whisky bottle*)
I'm gonna just sit here and drain this bottle. And when I've drunk the last drop, if I still feel then the way I feel now, I'm gonna take this bottle and break it over his melon head.

JACOB

Before we stepped in here, you told all of us to be cool. That means you, too.

SETH
(*tossing it off*)
I never said do what I do, I said do what I say.

JACOB

Are you so much of a fucking loser, you can't tell when you've won?

Richard, Kate and Scott both turn to Jacob. Nobody can believe what he just said. Neither can Seth who calmly lays down his drinking glass.

SETH

What did you call me?

JACOB

Nothing. I didn't make a statement. I asked a question. Would you like me to ask it again? Very well. Are you such a loser you can't tell when you've won?
(*pause*)

The entire state of Texas, along with the FBI, is looking for you. Did they find you? No. They couldn't. They had every entrance to the border covered. There's no way you could get across. Did you? Yes, you did. You've won, Seth, enjoy it.

Seth looks at Jacob, then picks up the bottle.

SETH

Jacob, I want you to have a drink with me. I insist.

Jacob slides his empty glass over to Seth. Seth pours booze in Jacob's glass and his own. Both men pick up the glasses.

To your family.

JACOB

To yours.

They both knock 'em back and slap the empty glasses down.

Now, is your shit together?

SETH

Forever together.

CUT TO:

Razor Charlie behind the bar grabs the greasy microphone that he uses to announce dancers.

RAZOR CHARLIE
(announcer voice; in Spanish)

And now for your viewing pleasure. The Mistress of the Macabre. The Epitome of Evil. The most sinister woman to dance on the face of the earth. Lowly dogs, get on your knees, bow your heads and worship at the feet of Santanico Pandemonium!

The lights go down low.

A light hits the stage.

The crowd hushes.

And on the stage steps Santanico Pandemonium.

This Mexican goddess is beautiful, but not the beauty that Stendhal described in 'As the Promise of Happiness', but the beauty of the siren

75

who lures men to their doom.

She dances to the raunchy music, not as if she owns the stage, but as if she owns the world. And if the patrons of the Titty Twister are her world, the world is proud to be her possession.

All activity in the bar, save Santanico, stops.

Even the Fuller/Gecko table falls under her spell. Especially Richard, Scott and Kate.

Santanico lays across one of the giant stone snakes. Fire shoots out of the snake's mouth.

When the music builds to its explosive section, Santanico leaps from the stage, landing in the middle of the room.

She does an eyes-closed voodoo dance in perfect step with the beat.

As the last verse plays, Santanico, like a snake, comes up from the ground, on top of the Fuller/Gecko table.

Richard, Kate and Scott are enraptured.

Santanico scans the table, zeroing in on our boy Richard. She stands over him.

While moving her body to the music, she lifts up the whisky bottle from the table, and pours the whisky down her leg.

She lifts up her foot, with the whisky dripping from her toes, and sticks it in Richard's face.

SANTANICO
(*to Richard; in Spanish*)

Drink up.

Richard, mesmerized, sucks the whisky off her toes.

The crowd goes wild.

Santanico smiles, mistress of all she surveys.

Jacob and Scott are embarrassed.

Richard continues to suck her toes.

The song ends; Santanico extracts her foot from Richard's mouth. Steps off the table. Takes a drink of whisky. Looks down at the seated Richard. She grabs the back of his hair, yanks his head back.

His mouth opens because she's hurting him.

She leans her face over his, as if she's going to kiss him, then lets the whisky from her mouth fall into his. They never touch.

The crowd applauds.

She lets go of Richard's hair. Except for Jacob and Richard, for their own reasons, the table applauds, none louder than Seth.

SETH

Bravo! Bravo! Bravo! Now that's what I call a fuckin' show!

One of Santanico's flunkies brings the naked woman a robe, which she puts on.

As the music continues to play, a very fucked-up looking Chet Pussy walks in. He goes over to Razor Charlie and points at Seth's table, describing what happened.

Seth notices Razor Charlie, Big Emilio and Chet moving rapidly towards their table.

Richard. Get on the clock.

Razor Charlie approaches.

> **RAZOR CHARLIE**
> (*to Chet; in Spanish*)

Which one?

> **CHET**
> (*pointing to Seth*)

This piece of shit broke my finger and my nose . . .

> (*pointing to Richard*)

. . . then this fag kicked me in the ribs while I was down.

That's all Big Emilio has to hear. He leans in with his beefy hand, grabs Richard by the shoulder.

> **BIG EMILIO**
> (*to the Gecko brothers*)

Up!

> **RICHARD**

Fuck off, ape man!

Razor Charlie whips out a knife and shoves it into Richard's hand.

Seth jumps to his feet and fires a round from his .45 into Big Emilio, sending his bullet-ridden body to the floor.

Richard grabs the knife and stabs Razor Charlie several times, taking him to the ground.

Jacob and his children have also hit the floor to stay out of gunfire.

The bikers, truckers, waitresses and whores all stop what they were doing.

Richard stands in bloody triumph and stabs the wooden table with the bloody knife.

The music continues to play, though the dancers stop dancing.

Santanico, who's closest to the two brothers, smells something.

Her nostrils flare.

Richard moves to his brother.

RICHARD

Are you okay?

SETH

Whatever.

Seth looks up and sees Chet still standing there.

You thought it was pretty funny, didn't you?

Both brothers fire on Chet.

Chet's blown left . . . right . . . left . . . right . . . then drops.

They point their guns towards the crowd.

Everybody be cool, or you'll be just as dead as these fucks!

Slow motion: blood drips down Richard's hand.

Slow motion: it splatters to the floor.

The camera scans the crowd. The patrons are scared, but the waitresses, whores and dancers lick their lips.

We move into Santanico's face. A special aroma fills her nostrils. Her eyes lock on Richard. The look on her face could easily be read as intense sexual desire.

Close-up: Kate on floor. She looks up and watches, eyes wide with fear, Santanico's transformation.

Santanico's nose recedes into her face like a rodent's.

The whites of her eyes turn yellow.

The fangs of a beast protrude from her mouth.

Kate yells from the floor.

KATE
(*yelling*)

Richie, look out!

Before Richard can turn around.

Santanico leaps across the floor, lands on his back and sinks her fangs into Richard's wounded shoulder.

Richard lets loose with an agonizing scream.

Seth turns to his brother's cry.

He sees Santanico Pandemonium, like a mongoose attached to a cobra, legs wrapped around Richard's waist, fangs buried deep in his shoulder, and Richard screaming and slamming about, trying to knock her off.

Richard screams to Seth:

RICHARD

Shoot her! Shoot her! Get her off!

Seth tries to aim his gun, but there's too much movement. He can't get a clear shot.

Jacob and his children can't believe what they're seeing.

Richard can't take it anymore, his knees buckle. Santanico rides him down to the floor.

Seth gets a clear shot, he takes aim and fires, hitting the vamp in the head, blowing her off his brother.

*Richard, who's on all fours, tries to stand and gets about half way
before he stops, saying:*

> RICHARD
> (*with his dying breath*)

Fucking bitch!

He tumbles over, a corpse.

> SETH

Richie.

*Suddenly, the eyes of Big Emilio, Razor Charlie and Chet Pussy pop
open. The 'dead' men sit up with evil grins on their faces.*

The patrons scream.

*A whore locks the front door with a complicated lock with steel rods
going into the ground, then turns toward the bar and yells:*

> WHORE

Dinner is served!

*The bikers and truckers who have been transfixed, watching the
impossible, realize that the waitresses, naked dancers and whores who
they were pawing just five minutes ago, have turned into yellow-eyed,
razor-fanged, drool-dripping vampires.*

The vamps attack.

What follows is a shark feeding frenzy.

*Whores, who had been sitting on customers' laps, sink their teeth into
unshaven necks.*

*One of the dancers has half her face concealed with a hand fan, then
pulls it away to reveal her evil-fanged grin. She whips the fan at her
date's throat, slitting it instantly. She drinks heavily from his neck.*

*One of the women turns into Mouth Vamp and shoves her tongue
down a patron's throat.*

*A screen dancer turns into a monster and bites her patron in half. She
walks out and suddenly weighs 300 pounds.*

A pool table vamp turns and bites the head off of the trucker teaching her pool.

Frost looks up and notices his girl is also a vamp, he jumps back and starts to fight.

Vamp girls fly out of the niche and attack Frost's comrades.

Naked strippers and bikers beat the shit out of each other.

Truckers get their heads caved in by women half their size.

The patrons use whatever they can find to fend off the monsters: chairs, chair legs, broken bottles, switchblades, anything.

Jacob, Kate and Scott make a dash and dive behind the bar. They hide and watch.

Behind him, Santanico lies next to the dead Richard. Her eyes pop open. She slithers around and rises up in her snake-like way.

Seth stays where he is, limp dick of a .45 in his hand, too freaked, scared and stunned to do anything. He stands motionless, watching what he can't believe.

Mouth Vamp walks towards him, having just bit into a lap dancer

customer's neck. The vamp walks right for Seth. She grabs another patron and pushes his head down to her belly. The belly opens up and devours the patron's head. She drops his lifeless corpse to the ground and continues towards Seth.

Seth starts to back up and runs right into Santanico.

SANTANICO
Let's see if you taste as good as your brother.

She approaches Seth, who fires at her. Bam . . . bam . . . bam . . . Click . . . click . . . click . . . click. She laughs and gives her hair a toss back. Seth, moving backwards, is terrified.

Santanico gives Seth a swinging roundhouse punch to the jaw that sends him flying over a table, sliding across the floor and into the wall.

A bad-ass biker named Sex-Machine leaps to the pool table and starts swinging a pool cue, left to right, fending off vamps like in a Jackie Chan routine. He breaks one upside Olympia Vamp's head and stakes her with it. He realizes the usefulness of the cue sticks and grabs a bunch of them off the rack, and throws them to his comrades below.

Big Emilio picks up the biker who stabbed him with a switchblade and throws the poor bastard from one end of the bar to the other. A few strippers are waiting for him and eat hungrily when he arrives.

Frost goes head-to-head with a stripper.

The vamp might have superhuman strength, but Frost has close to superhuman strength, and he's matching the vamp bitch blow for blow.

Frost grabs her by the waist, lifts her up over his head and brings her down hard on an upturned table, impaling her on the wooden leg. He realizes that with four legs he can manage three more vamps and continues to drop the vamps onto the table until, with a top shot, a Busky Berkeley arrangement of vamp corpses is revealed.

Sex-Machine is still swinging his pool cue, when Razor Charlie appears, by way of the chandelier, knife in hand.

Sex-Machine jumps off the table to meet the challenge. Razor Charlie swings at him, Sex-Machine leaps back, swinging his pool cue at him. They do this dance until Sex whips Charlie with his whip, pulling him down to the pool table, then cracks Charlie across the chest with the pool cue, breaking it in half. Charlie feels the hit. Sex plunges the splintered end of the cue into Razor Charlie's heart, removes his whip and walks away as Charlie screams the vampire's death scream, and melts into the pool table.

Seth comes to and finds Santanico standing over him. He tries to rise, but Santanico places her bare foot on his chest, pinning him down to the floor. He tries to move, but the pressure of her foot is equivalent to an engine block placed on his chest.

SANTANICO

I'm not gonna drain you completely. You're gonna turn for me. You'll be my slave. You'll live for me. You'll eat bugs because I order it. Because I don't think you're worthy of human blood, you'll feed on the blood of stray dogs. You'll be my foot stool. And at my command, you'll lick the dog shit from my boot heel. Since you'll be my dog, your new name will be Spot. Welcome to slavery.

Seth aims his .45 and fires. The chandelier above her plunges down on top of her.

Santanico is hit in the chest. She falls to the ground, melts into it. Seth walks over and kicks the chandelier over. She's gone.

Big Emilio sees Santanico's fiery death. He lets out a cry.

BIG EMILIO

Noooooo!

He turns his hateful gaze on the two humans.

Seth and Jacob see Big Emilio zeroing in on them. Then they see him move his big frame in their direction. Seth turns to Jacob.

SETH

We may be in trouble.

Big Emilio walks steadily through the bar like Godzilla through Tokyo, tipping over tables, knocking fighting vamps and humans alike on their asses on his way to stamp out Seth and Jacob. A trucker jumps in his path to attack him, with a quick swing of his hand the trucker is brushed aside, receiving a broken neck for the effort.

Big Emilio neither breaks his stride nor takes his eyes off Seth and Jacob.

Seth and Jacob both grab pieces of wood, holding them like weapons, but the wood looks puny compared with their opponent.

Big Emilio stands in front of them.

The two men hold their wood tight.

Fangs grow in Big Emilio's mouth that make him look like a huge walking shark.

Just when Big Emilo's ready to strike, he hears behind him:

> VOICE
> (*off-screen*)

Hey, you, monkey man!

Big Emilio turns and sees Sex-Machine across the room.

> SEX-MACHINE

Anything you gotta say to them, say to him first.
> (*pointing to Frost*)

Both Seth and Jacob attack Big Emilio from behind. He knocks them away effortlessly.

They both hit the ground.

Frost gestures with his hand to Big Emilio to 'come ahead'.

Big Emilio charges towards Frost, like a runaway locomotive.

Frost walks casually towards Emilio, waiting for impact.

The two huge men collide.

What follows is literally a war of the gargantuans. The two mastiffs pound each other. Finally, Big Emilio buckles first and hits the floor.

Once on the floor, Seth and Jacob, stand over the huge vamp, beating him with clubs and pipes, like LA's finest. The vamp can do nothing except squirm on the floor from the savage beating.

FROST

That's enough.

Jacob and Seth stop.

Sex-Machine holds a pool cue in his hand. He snaps off the end tip, making it jagged like a spear, sticks it into the big vamp's fallen body. Big Emilio, screams, twitches and dies. The pool cue sticks out straight up from the dead vamp.

Chet Pussy espies Kate, Ms Apple Pie Pussy herself. He breaks into a lecherous grin and licks the blood from around his mouth.

Kate and Scott are cowering behind the bar when Chet appears over the top. They both let out a scream. Scott goes to protect his sister and receives a punch in the face for his trouble. Chet dives at Kate.

CHET

You know what everybody says about me? I suck!

Chet goes to bite Kate, grabbing at her T-shirt, and sees her crucifix. He recoils. Scott grabs hold of his head from behind. Kate jumps up from the floor, rips off her cross and grabs Chet by his beatnik beard, opening his mouth. She shoves the cross inside. Chet's eyes roll up back into his head. Scott slaps Chet hard on the back.

GULP.

Chet has swallowed the crucifix. A sizzling sound is heard moving down from his throat to his belly. He opens his mouth and melts down to a skeleton. The eyeballs are still intact, and he looks at himself before locking eyes one last time with Kate. Then his eyes explode and he falls over.

By this time there are not too many people left. Most of the vampires have been killed by wooden stakes and most of the customers have been butchered or drained.

All that's left on the vampire side are two naked dancers and two whores. On the human side are Seth, Jacob and his kids, Sex-

Machine and Frost. Aside from the children, who are hiding behind the bar, all the humans are holding wooden stakes.

The four human men group together. The four female vampires charge, teeth exposed, snarling and dripping with blood. Seth, Jacob, Sex-Machine and Frost raise their weapons and slam, almost simultaneously, the four vamps. All four staked bodies hit the floor.

Kate and Scott run from behind the bar to their father's side.

They all stand looking at the horrible carnage that has taken place. The floor is littered with dead bodies.

FROST

Ain't they supposed to burn up or something?

At that moment a bright flash erupts, illuminating everyone's face. The sound of quick-burning flames fills the air. Everybody shields their eyes from the intense light, which lasts only a split second.

It vanishes, along with the bodies of the vampires. All that remains is a smoldering mess of goo where the bodies once lay.

The band is still playing. So Sex-Machine and Frost go to kill the band. The band says goodnight and explodes.

They all stare at the mess for a few seconds and then run for the door. It's locked. They bang on the door, but it's useless. It ain't budging, yet they all continue banging . . .

. . . except for Seth. He walks over to his dead brother's body and kneels beside it.

He takes his hand.

> SETH

Richie, I'm sorry I fucked things up. You'd have really liked it in El Ray. We'd have found peace there. I love you little brother, I'll miss ya bad.

Seth goes to kiss his brother's lips when Richard's eyes pop open. They're yellow. Seth raises his head in surprise.

> RICHARD

I'm glad you feel that way, Seth. I love you, too.

Richard grabs Seth by the front of his shirt and pulls him down to him. Fangs are now exposed. Seth tries to pull away. He screams for the others to help. Richard pulls Seth down to striking distance and opens his mouth to take the big bite, when Sex-Machine grabs Seth from behind and yanks him from Richard's grasp. Jacob, Frost and the kids have surrounded Richard and proceed to kick him and stomp his head. Sex-Machine picks up a chair and smashes it against a wall. He picks up one of the chair legs and walks over to where the others are holding Richard down. Richard sees the wood in the biker's hand. He knows what that means. Seth whips out his .45 and points it at Sex-Machine.

> SETH

Touch my brother with that stake, biker, and vampires won't need to suck your blood, they'll be able to lick it up off the floor.

> SEX-MACHINE

He ain't your brother no more.

> SETH

That's a matter of opinion, and I don't give a fuck about yours.

Jacob, Frost and the kids continue to hold Richard down to the ground.

Don't be an idiot, he'll kill us all!

Seth aims his gun at the group.

SETH

Shut up!

Richard's giggling.

RICHARD

Yeah, shut up.

Seth, still holding the outstretched gun, takes the stake out of Sex-Machine's hand. Seth lowers the .45.

SETH

Hold him down.

The smile evaporates from Richard's face.

Richie, here's the peace in death I could never give you in life.

Seth puts the stake over Richard's heart. Using the butt of his .45 like a hammer, he pounds the stake into Richard's heart. Richard screams and dies. They all stand around the body as it bursts into flames and disintegrates into goo. Seth breaks away from the group and walks over to the bar. He grabs a bottle of whisky and starts downing it. Kate, of all people, walks away from the group and joins Seth at the bar.

KATE

Are you okay?

SETH

Peachy! Why shouldn't I be? The world's my oyster, except for the fact that I just rammed a wooden stake in my brother's heart because he turned into a vampire, even though I don't believe in vampires. Aside from that unfortunate business, everything's hunky-dory.

KATE

I'm really sorry.

SETH

Bullshit! You hate us. If you had half a chance you'd feed us to them!

JACOB

Then why didn't I?

Jacob walks over to Seth.

I saved your life. I didn't have to, but I did. And I'm sorry you lost your brother. I'm sorry he's dead. I'm sorry everybody's dead. Now, if we're gonna get out of this we need each other. And we need you sober and thinking, not drunk and . . .

As Jacob has been talking, a sound has started that has grown louder and louder. Jacob stops in mid-sentence to identify it.

What the hell is that?

FROST

At first I just thought it was birds.

SEX-MACHINE

No, it's more of a gnawing sound. Birds peck, they don't gnaw. Rats gnaw.

Seth puts the bottle in his hand down.

SETH

It's bats.

EXT. TITTY TWISTER — NIGHT

The outside of the Titty Twister is literally covered with bats, clawing, flapping, gnawing, trying like hell to get inside.

INT. TITTY TWISTER — NIGHT

Everybody listens to the bats scratching and clawing all along the walls, the roof and at the front door. Everyone's scared shitless and nobody has the slightest idea what to do next. The door begins to crack and splinter, little claws poke their way through.

JACOB

Give me a hand!

Jacob runs to a table top. He grabs it and covers the area the bats are trying to claw through. The others grab other items to help secure and barricade the door.

As the survivors are boarding up the door and the windows in panic, a dead biker that the vampires fed on pops open his yellow eyes. He sits up and sees all the furious activity. Everyone's so busy they don't notice their new friend. The dead biker vamp sets his sights on Kate, who's putting a board into place. He springs to his feet and pounces on her, just as Sex-Machine turns from across the room in her direction.

SEX-MACHINE

Watch out, girly!

The biker vamp grabs Kate from behind. She lets out a scream. The vamp holds her close to him in a bear hug, but she's moving around so much he can't get a clear bite. The others hear the scream and look toward Kate. Sex-Machine, Big Emilio's baseball bat in hand, is halfway to the rescue. As the biker vamp opens his mouth to take a juicy bite out of Kate's shoulder, Kate rams her head back, hitting the vamp in the mouth and breaking his fangs. He releases her and spits out his teeth just as Sex-Machine runs up and swings the baseball bat upside the vamp's head, breaking the bat in two and sending the vamp to the floor. As the vamp lies on the floor seeing stars, Sex-Machine grabs one of the broken ends of the bat and shoves it into the vamp's heart. He dies and bursts into flames.

At that point, three other dead victims rise to a sitting position. Sex-Machine grabs a chair and throws it to the ground, breaking it. He grabs the four legs.

(mumbling to himself)

Goddamn fuckin' vampires.

He turns into Captain Sex-Machine, Vampire Hunter. He stakes two of the vampires as they get to their feet. Both spew green blood, scream, die and burst into flames. The third, a trucker vampire wearing a CAT Cap, smacks Sex-Machine in the mouth, which sends him for a loop.

As CAT Cap runs toward the fallen Sex-Machine, Kate jumps on his back from behind. Both of them go tumbling into a stack of whisky cases. Sex-Machine runs over and grabs Kate by the hand, pulling her up and out of the way. CAT Cap is lying in a pile of broken bottles and whisky. Sex-Machine raises his stake as CAT Cap dies and drives it in the vamp's black heart. CAT Cap dies and bursts into flames, which ignites the whisky, starting a giant fire.

> SEX-MACHINE

Fire!

Frost and Jacob stop barricading and run to the fire.

> FROST
> (*to Sex-Machine*)

We'll put this out. You stake the rest of these fuckers.

> SEX-MACHINE

Way ahead of ya.

> (*to Kate*)

What's your name, girly?

> KATE

Kate, what's yours?

> SEX-MACHINE

Sex-Machine. Pleased to meetcha. Kate, let's stake these blood-sucker fuckers.

Kate and Sex-Machine give each other a high five and go to work staking the dead bodies.

Jacob and Frost beat down the fire with their jackets and whatever else is at hand.

A hole begins to appear where a window had been plastered over. Little claws scrape their way through. Scott stands in front of the window.

> SCOTT
> (*yelling*)

We got a problem!

Seth, who is barricading doors and windows, looks in Scott's direction. The hole in the plaster cracks open and out pops a little, fleshy vampire bat/rat head. The bat/rat, which is squeaking and hissing its head off, tries to squeeze its body through the newly formed hole.

Seth, gun in hand, runs to the window. He points the .45, point-blank range at the head of the bat/rat.

The bat/rat sees this, makes an 'oh shit' face and yanks his head back through the hole.

Seth, ready to fire, lowers his gun in bewilderment, when . . .

WHAM!

The bat/rat bursts through the hole, like shot out of a cannon, hitting Seth in the gut and sending him flying, landing hard on his back.

Once Seth hits the ground, the bat-thing (which has the body of a fat rat with a bat's large wingspan) lickety-split runs up Seth's body to his jugular. Seth's hand grabs the bat's neck, and tries to push it away. But the bat-thing has its claws dug in Seth's clothes. The bat-thing is just inches from Seth's face. Its mouth is snapping.

SETH

Get this bastard off of me!

Frost leaves Jacob with the fire, comes from behind, grabs the bat-thing and yanks it off of Seth.

Sex-Machine and Kate are green, bloody mess from their preventive staking of dead bodies. Sex-Machine kneels by a dead body, raising the stake in his hand to spear him. The body springs up and bites Sex-Machine on the arm. Red blood squirts everywhere. Sex-Machine screams, then brings the stake down in the body's chest. It dies, burns and turns into goo. Sex-Machine holds his arm and wraps it with a piece of his shirt. He quickly looks around to see if anybody saw him get bit. Nobody saw it, everybody was too busy.

Frost holds the flapping, fighting, snapping bat-thing in front of him at arm's length. He struggles with it for awhile, then . . .

. . . bashes its head against the bar. The first bash takes some fight out of the little fucker, so Frost bashes its head against the bar six or seven times. He then throws the bat-thing on the bar, turns it over, grabs a pencil from a cup next to the register, and rams it in the bat-

*thing's heart. The bat-thing coughs and dies. There's a flash of
flames, followed by a pile of goo.*

*Sex-Machine and Kate cover up a hole in the plastered-up window
with a table while Frost, Scott and Seth wrestle with the bat-thing.*

Jacob has put out the fire.

*Everybody comes together, exhausted, and takes a breather. Outside,
the bats continue to try and claw their way in.*

JACOB

Is everybody okay?

Everyone mutters 'yeah'.

Okay, does anybody here know what's going on?

SETH

Yeah, I know what's going on. We got a bunch of fuckin' vampires
outside trying to get inside and suck our fuckin' blood! That's it,
plain and simple. And I don't wanna hear any bullshit about 'I
don't believe in vampires' because I don't fuckin' believe in
vampires either. But I do believe in my own two fuckin' eyes, and
with my two eyes I saw fuckin' vampires! Now, does everybody
agree we're dealin' with vampires.

Everybody agrees.

You too, preacher?

JACOB

I'm like you. I don't believe in vampires, but I believe in what I
saw.

SETH

Good for you. Now, since we all believe we're dealing with
vampires, what do we know about vampires? Crosses hurt
vampires. Do you have a cross?

JACOB

In the Winnebago.

SETH

In other words, no.

96

SCOTT

What are you talking about? We got crosses all over the place. All you gotta do is put two sticks together and you got a cross.

SEX-MACHINE

He's right. Peter Cushing does that all the time.

SETH

I don't know about that. In order for it to have any power, I think it's gotta be an official crucifix.

JACOB

What's an official cross? Some piece of tin made in Taiwan? What makes that official? If a cross works against vampires, it's not the cross itself, it's what the cross represents. The cross is a symbol of holiness.

SETH

Okay, I'll buy that. So we got crosses covered, moving right along, what else?

FROST

Wooden stakes in the heart been workin' pretty good so far.

SEX-MACHINE

Garlic, holy water, sunlight . . . I forget, does silver do anything to a vampire?

SCOTT

That's werewolves.

SEX-MACHINE

I know silver bullets are werewolves. But I'm pretty sure silver has some sort of effect on vampires.

KATE

Does anybody have any silver?

No.

Then who cares?

SCOTT

When's sunrise?

Jacob looks at his watch.

                    JACOB
About two hours from now.

                    KATE
So all we have to do is get by for a few more hours and then we
can walk right out the front door.

                  SEX-MACHINE
Yeah, that's true. But I doubt our barricades, that door, those
plastered windows and these walls will last two more hours with
those bat fucks fuckin' with 'em.

                    JACOB
Has anybody here read a real book about vampires, or are we just
remembering what a movie said? I mean a real book.

                  SEX-MACHINE
You mean like a Time-Life book?

Everybody laughs.

                    FROST
               (*in a cowboy voice*)
John Wesley Hardin, so mean he once shot a man for snorin'.

                    JACOB
I take it the answer's no. Okay then, what do we know about these
vampires?

                    SETH
Aside from that they're thirsty.

                    FROST
Well, one thing, they might have superhuman strength, but you
can hurt 'em.

                    JACOB
Yeah, that bottle upside the head of Santanico didn't kill her, but
it didn't feel too good either.

                  SEX-MACHINE
Another thing, you try and ram a broken chair leg in a human, you
better be one strong son-of-a-bitch. The human body is one

rough-tough machine. But these vamps got soft bodies. The texture of their skin is softer, mushier. You can push shit right through 'em. Conceivably, if you hit one hard enough, you could take their fuckin' head off.

SCOTT

You could take their head off.

SETH

Actually, our best weapon against these satanic cocksuckers is this man.

He points at Jacob.

He's a preacher.

Frost and Sex-Machine look toward Jacob.

As far as God's concerned, we might just as well be a piece of fuckin' shit. But he's one of the boys. Only one problem, his faith ain't what it used to be.

Jacob punches Seth in the mouth, sending him to the floor. Jacob stands over him.

JACOB

I've had enough of your taunts.

Seth looks up from the floor.

SETH

I'm not taunting you. We need you. A faithless preacher doesn't mean shit to us. But a man who's a servant of God can grab a cross, shove it in these monsters' asses. A servant of God can bless the tap water and turn it into a weapon.

Seth rises.

I know why you lost your faith. How could true holiness exist if your wife can be taken away from you and your children? Now, I always said God can kiss my fuckin' ass. Well, I changed my lifetime tune about thirty minutes ago 'cause I know, without a doubt, what's out there trying to get in here is pure evil straight from hell. And if there is a hell, and those monsters are from it, there's got to be a heaven. Now which are you, a faithless

99

preacher or a mean, motherfuckin' servant of God?

Jacob has to laugh at that. So does everybody else. Jacob sticks out his hand and shakes Seth's.

JACOB

I'm a mean, motherfuckin' servant of God.

The laughter and good humor passes quickly and the only sound to be heard is that of the bats' gnawing and clawing. It immediately reminds the group of the deep, deep shit they're in.

KATE

I don't know if I can take two hours of that noise.

FROST

You can. You'll take it 'cause ya got no choice. How'd ya like twenty-four hours of it, lying in a muddy ditch with only the rotting corpses of your friends to keep you company?

JACOB

What are you talking about?

FROST

Back in '72 I was in 'Nam, trapped behind enemy lines, lying in a rat hole with my entire squad dead. They thought they killed everybody, and, except for me, they were right. But it wasn't for lack of trying. A grenade blew up right next to me, that's why I'm so pretty. They thought I was dead, so I played dead. They dumped all the bodies in a ditch. All I could do was lie there playing possum. Dead bodies under me, dead bodies on top of me, listening to the enemy laugh and joke hour after hour after hour . . .

As Frost goes into his monologue, the sound fades out and the camera moves to Sex-Machine. He's having a hot flush. He can't hear anything. He's looking at Frost speaking, but he doesn't hear any sound. Then he hears a deep, male voice say:

MALE VOICE
(*voice-over*)

Thirst.

'Who the fuck was that?' he thinks to himself. He turns around:

nobody's there. No one else in the group seems to hear it. A female voice says seductively:

> FEMALE VOICE
> (*voice-over*)

Thirst.

We hear Sex-Machine's thoughts in voice-over.

> SEX-MACHINE
> (*voice-over*)

Stop fucking saying that!

> TWO MALE VOICES
> (*voice-over*)

Thirst.

> SEX-MACHINE
> (*voice-over*)

That bite weren't nothin'. It just hurt like a son-of-a-bitch, that's all. It barely punched the skin.

Sex-Machine looks at Frost, who's acting out his story. The biker is miming fighting and slashing. As he continues to describe we hear nothing. All we hear are many voices, male, female, children saying:

> VOICES
> (*voice-over*)

Thirst . . . Thirst . . . Thirst . . .

Sex-Machine begins to look at the other members of the group in a thirsty way. He stares at each of their necks, closer and closer until he can see the veins on Frost's neck actually pulsating, throbbing, beckoning to him. Sex-Machine has turned into a vampire.

The sound comes back as Frost finishes his story.

> FROST

. . . and then when I came back to my senses, I realized I had killed the entire V.C. Squadron singlehandedly. My bayonet had blood and chunks of yellow flesh on it like some cannibal's shish kebab. And to this day I don't have the slighest idea how I –

Sex-Machine lets out a hideous cry.

THIRST!

Frost screams as Sex-Machine grabs hold of him and bites into his neck.

The group tries to pull the two men apart.

Jacob gets his arm around Sex-Machine's neck and tries pulling.

Sex-Machine takes his teeth out of Frost's neck and sinks them in Jacob's arm.

Jacob screams and lets go.

Seth, Kate and Scott react to Jacob being bit.

Sex-Machine grabs Jacob and tosses him effortlessly over the bar; he crashes into a shelf full of liquor bottles.

Frost hops around the room, mad as a hornet, holding his bleeding neck.

FROST

I been bit! He fuckin' bit me!

Sex-Machine punches Seth in the face, dropping him like a sack of potatoes.

He smacks the shit out of Kate. She goes flying into a table.

Sex-Machine turns and sees Frost breaking off a big table leg. Frost looks at the big vamp.

(*to Sex-Machine*)
You're dead, motherfucker! You're gonna bite me! You just turned me into a vampire, asshole!

SEX-MACHINE
What are you gonna do about it?

Frost, table leg in hand, runs, screaming his head off, straight at Sex-Machine.

Sex-Machine's nostrils flare. He raises his meaty fist and pulls it back, so he can really haul off.

Frost, top speed, stake raised, screaming.

Sex-Machine lets loose with his punch.

Seth, Scott and Kate look up from the floor.

Jacob rises from behind the bar.

Frost's face collides with Sex-Machine's fist. Sex-Machine hits Frost so hard it lifts the biker off the ground and propels him through the air.

Seth sees where Frost is heading and says:

SETH
Oh shit!

Jacob sees.

JACOB
Good lord!

Frost, in mid-air, hits the barricaded, plastered-over window and crashes through it.

Sex-Machine lets loose with a maniacal laugh.

Hundreds of bat-things fly into the bar.

Seth grabs the two kids by the hand and runs for the back room.

Behind the bar, Jacob grabs two pieces of wood from off the ground.

Ten bat-things are in hot pursuit of Seth, Kate and Scott, who are running for their lives. They get to the door of the back room, whip it open, dive in and slam it behind them. An ugly, fleshy bat-thing manages to get its head caught in the door as it closes. Kate and Scott push on the door as hard as they can. The bat-thing's head, which is inside, screams, howls and snaps in fury.

Seth turns toward the bat/vamp in the door. He sticks his .45 in its big mouth.

SETH

You wanna suck something, suck on this!

He fires four shots that blow the bat vamp's head all over the wall.

Kate yells:

KATE

We have to go back for Daddy!

SETH

Daddy's dead.

KATE

Noooo!

She spins and grabs the door knob, ready to fling the door and help her father. Scott grabs her and pushes her up against the wall.

SCOTT

He's right, Kate. Daddy's dead! He was too far away. If flinging that door and filling this room with those bat-things would save him, I'd fling it. The only thing it'll do is turn us into one of them.

KATE

He needs our help!

SCOTT

He's beyond our help. You saw him get bit. I saw him get bit. We

all saw it. You can't help him. I've got no one left to lose but you. I can't be alone again. We're sticking together.

Just then they hear Jacob's voice booming from the bar-room.

INT. BAR-ROOM – NIGHT

Jacob, holding a cross made out of two sticks and reciting appropriate verse from the Bible, is keeping the vampires at bay. But, as Seth predicted, it is the shining power of his restored faith that is his mightiest weapon. Jacob is making his way through the vampires, toward the back door. A lot of the bats have transformed into bat/devil/human creatures.

The creatures stand at the edge of Jacob's force-field of holiness. Many bat-things fly around the bar like mad, whirling dervishes. A cluster of bat-things fly over, above and in front of Jacob. They all growl and hiss at the man of God. For every one step forward Jacob takes, the vampires take one step back. Jacob recites the verse from the Bible in a threatening, mean, motherfucking, servant of God tone. As he speaks with authority and strength, he sees Frost lying on the ground, bat-things on him like ants on a candy bar. But Jacob is too much in control to let even this repugnant sight trip him up.

Jacob has backed himself up by the door.

> JACOB

Open the door.

The door flies open. Jacob jumps inside. The door slams shut.

Jacob hugs daughter and son. As he hugs them, we see his bloody arm.

When he releases them, they can't help but notice.

> SETH

Did he . . .?

> JACOB

Yep.

Seth explodes, knocking over boxes, busting chairs, tipping over tables and cussing a blue streak.

SETH

Fuck, piss, shit! Motherfuckin' vampires! Motherfuckin' vampires! *Goddamn motherfuckin' vampires!*

Seth runs over to the barricaded door and yells to the creatures on the other side.

You all are gonna fuckin' die! I'm gonna fuckin' kill every last one of you godless pieces of shit!

JACOB
(*to Seth*)

You bet your sweet ass you are, and I'm gonna help you do it. But we ain't got much time.

Kate is crying, she knows what's happened to her father.

KATE

You're gonna be okay, aren't you Daddy?

JACOB

No, I'm not. I've been bit. In effect, I'm already dead.

Scott and Kate, crying, grab their father and hold on for dear life. Jacob wants to cry, but if he breaks down, the kids will never have the courage for what they must do.

(*to his children*)

Children, listen to me. I love you two more than anybody. And I just want you to know you've made me proud all your lives. But never more so than tonight. And I wish we could sit here and cry till I pass on, but we can't. Because I'm not going to pass on. I'm going to turn into a monster. And when I do, I'm going to be dangerous. But before that happens, just know I love you.

(*to Seth and the kids*)

Now, I'd say in the next twenty or thirty minutes our friends outside will bust in this door. And I'll probably turn into a vampire within the hour. Now, you have two choices. You can wait for me to turn, then deal with me, then wait for them to burst inside here and the three of you will deal with them. Or, we can kick open that door and the four of us can hit 'em with everything we have, and carve a path right through 'em to the front entrance. But if we're gonna go at 'em, we gotta go at 'em now. I confused them, I scared them, I took them off guard. But they're going to get unconfused, they're going to get unscared, they're going to get together and they're going to hit that door like a ton of bricks. And when that moment arrives, we gotta be ready.

Jacob sees that the back room is pretty damn big and filled with boxes and crates.

JACOB

What's this stuff?

SETH

My guess is that this little dive's been feeding on nomad road waifs like bikers and truckers for a long time. This is probably some of the shipments they stole off the trucks.

JACOB

Well, I say let's tear this place apart for weapons. So when they burst through that door, we'll make 'em wish they never did.

SETH

I don't give a shit about living or dying anymore. I just want to send as many of these devils back to hell as I can.

JACOB

Amen.

MONTAGE

The survivors are opening boxes and prying open crates. A lot of what they find is bullshit. Pantyhose, coffee, Teddy bears, etc. But a few of the boxes are just what the doctor ordered. Cases from a sporting goods supplier yield a shipment of baseball bats. Meant to arrive at toy stores are a shipment of Uzi replica squirt guns and a box of balloons. And captured en route to a hardware store are shipments of power tools, saws and jackhammers.

Seth and Scott saw the bats into wooden stakes.

Kate fills the Uzi squirt guns with tap water from the back room sink.

Jacob, with Seth's knife, etches a cross into every bullet in the .45 automatic's last full clip of ammo.

108

Vampires all start converging on the back room door, getting their courage back.

Kate makes water balloons.

Seth attaches a wooden stake to the end of a jackhammer.

Jacob blesses the water in the squirt guns and balloons, turning it into holy water.

Our heroes work together, preparing for the battle to come. The back room door, barricaded with crates and boxes, begins to be pounded on by the undead on the other side. The room tone is a combination of chewing, scratching, pounding, squeaking and screaming.

Finally they're ready.

Jacob turns to his kids.

> JACOB
> Before we go any further, I need you three to promise me something. I'll fight with you to the bitter end, but when I turn into one of them, I won't be Jacob anymore. I'll be a lapdog of Satan. I want you three to promise you'll take me down, no different from the rest.

The kids can't say the words.

> SETH
> I promise.

> JACOB
> Kate, Scott?

> KATE
> I promise.

> JACOB
> Scott?

> SCOTT
> Yeah, I promise.

Jacob doesn't believe them.

JACOB

Why don't I believe you?

He picks up the .45.

I'm gonna ask you two again, then I want you to swear to God that you'll kill me. If you don't, I'm gonna just kill myself right now. Now, since you need me, I think you better swear. Kate, do you swear to God that when I turn into one of the undead, you'll kill me?

Kate doesn't answer. Jacob places the .45 barrel against his temple.

Kate, we don't have all day, so I'm only gonna count to five. One . . . two . . . three . . . four . . .

KATE

Okay, okay, I promise I'll do it!

JACOB

Not good enough, swear to God.

KATE

I swear to God, our Father, that when you change into one of the undead, I will kill you.

JACOB

Good girl. Now, Scott, we have even less time, so I'm only giving you the count of three. One . . .

SCOTT

You don't believe in suicide.

JACOB

It's not suicide if you're already dead. Two . . .

SCOTT

Okay, I'll kill you when you change, I swear to God in Jesus Christ's name.

JACOB

Thank you, son.

SETH

Okay, vampire killers, let's kill some fuckin' vampires.

INT. BAR-ROOM – NIGHT

The vampires, bat-things and what-have-you, start breaking down the door. They are in a mad frenzy. They burst through the door.

Waiting for them are Scott and Kate holding Uzi squirt guns and water balloons draped down their chests on a belt like grenades. Jacob is holding a cross made of sharp wooden stakes and the .45 with the cross bullets.

Seth is holding the jackhammer.

The survivors walk out of the back room into the bar. The vamps back up, letting them inside.

What we have here is a Mexican standoff, à la Wild Bunch. *A moment of peace before the battle. The vamps just watch the humans. The humans just watch the vamps. Then, like the bull in the china shop, Seth ends the peace by starting up the jackhammer.*

SETH

Kill 'em all!

Jacob holds up the cross, the vamps react.

The kids spray the crowd with Uzi fire, burning vampire flesh.

The pack of vamps retreat while the Fuller squad walk forward. They are attacked on all sides, but they keep moving toward the door.

Seth slams the stakes into several of the vamps, it speeds in and out of vampire chests, each time spraying him in green vamp blood.

Jacob shoves his cross stake into a vampire with one hand and shoots three vampires with blessed bullets with the other.

Flame bursts from the vampires' chests when the bullets hit.

Kate and Scott both whip water balloons off their belts and toss them into the crowd.

They burst and fry several of the vamps, who fall, screaming in pain.

From its perch on a wood ceiling beam, a bat-thing drops and hurls toward the group.

Jacob sees it, raises his gun and fires.

The bat-thing bursts into a ball of screaming fire.

Seth continues carving a path to the front door by slamming the hammer stake into vampire chests.

The front door is barricaded again by a big table and other junk.

SCOTT
(*yelling*)

Why did they block the door again?

JACOB
(*yelling*)

To keep the daylight out! This is where they sleep! Get to the door!

Seth tries to get to the front door, when Sex-Machine, now a half-bat, half-devil vamp, about six foot seven, drops from above in front of him. Seth rams the stake in its chest. The Sex-Machine-thing screams out, lifting the hammer and Seth off the ground.

Seth is thrown from his hold on the hammer across the room. He crashes into a table.

112

The Sex-Machine-thing falls back with the jackhammer sticking out of his chest, dead.

Kate, spraying Uzi fire like Rambo, sees Seth fall. She screams:

KATE

Seth!

Seth quickly gets up to find himself surrounded by vampires on all sides. With no weapons, he puts up on dukes.

SETH

Okay, deadboys, come on! Take a bite and feel all right!

Kate clusters with her father and Scott.

KATE
(yelling)

I'm going for 'em!

JACOB

No!

KATE

Everybody goes home!

Kate turns into a squirtgun-firing, water-balloon-throwing, one-woman army, as she breaks from her father and heads in Seth's direction.

(screaming)

Die, monster, die! Die, monster, die!

Kate mows down the group by Seth, they lie on the floor, burning in agony. Kate takes Seth's hand and gives him a couple of water balloons and a stake.

(to Seth)

Watch my back!

SETH

Anytime.

Cutting through vampires, the two make their way across the bar.

Jacob, firing the .45, takes out several more vampires in fiery death.

113

Scott fires the Uzi and chucks more water balloons.

As Jacob fights, all of a sudden the sound goes out. He can't hear anything. He wonders if he's gone deaf. He starts to hear the words: 'Thirst, thirst, thirst.' He notices the vampires have stopped attacking him. They look at him with happy smiles on their devilish faces. Fangs begin to grow. His eyes are yellow.

Scott turns to his dad. He sees his father is a monster.

Jacob, with a devilish grin on his face, grabs Scott and sinks his teeth into Scott's forearm. Scott screams bloody murder as his dad begins to drain him of blood.

Scott takes one of the water balloons he's wearing and smashes it against Jacob's head.

The holy water melts half of Jacob's face away. He lets go of Scott, screaming, and drops the .45 on the floor.

Scott drops to the ground, picking up the gun. He brings it up to fire.

A totally evil Jacob, with only half a face, matches stares with the boy he once called his son.

Scott's eyes turn to steel.

SCOTT

I swear to God, in Jesus Christ's name.

He fires, sending a holy bullet into Jacob's forehead, creating a hole from which fire shoots out. Jacob's entire head bursts into flames, then explodes.

From across the room, Kate sees her daddy ignite. She cries out. In the thick of the battle, Seth yells.

SETH

Fight now, cry later.

Kate takes his advice and hits a vamp square in the face with a holy water balloon, which melts his head.

A bat-thing lands on the back of Scott's neck. He screams as it bites into him. He drops the .45.

Kate sees Scott get bit.

KATE

Oh my God.

Another bat-thing lands on Scott's arm and takes a bite. Scott screams.

You bastards!

She goes to spray them when her Uzi runs out of water.

Now seven bat-things are on Scott, biting and sucking blood. Scott is in agony.

SCOTT

Kill me Kate!

Kate runs for her brother, does a dive and a roll, coming up by the .45, snatching it in one motion and firing three times.

One . . . two . . . three bat-things are hit, shoot flames, then all of them explode, blowing up Scott.

The remaining vamps approach.

All the humans have left is a few bullets and one holy balloon.

SETH

How many bullets left, kid?

KATE

Not many.

SETH

Well, when you run out of weapons, just start cold cocking 'em.
Make 'em sing for their supper.

The two survivors are backed up against a wall.

Two bat-things do a kamikaze dive from the air toward Seth.

Seth throws the holy balloon at them.

Direct hit. The two bat-things burst into flames and spiral to the floor.

*The two survivors look at the vampires, who stand before them. A
moment of stillness before the attack. Kate stands holding the .45,
arm outstretched.*

KATE
(*to Seth*)

Should I use the last bullets on us?

SETH

You use 'em on the first couple of these parasites that try to bite
you.

*The vamps begins to close in. Kate lines up the .45 sights on the face
of an approaching vampire.*

*Seth holds the Uzi like a club, ready to bash in the first vampire's
head that gets in swinging distance.*

*Beams of sunlight shoot through the holes that Kate shot through the
wall. Approaching vampires burn. The scorched vamps scream like
they've never screamed before.*

Shoot more holes!

*Kate turns away from the vamps and shoots holes in the wall behind
him. Daylight comes through, providing Kate and Seth with a safe,
lighted area.*

The .45's empty.

The vamps hiss and scream at the frustration of not being able to get at them.

The two survivors hold hands, when . . .

. . . all of a sudden the door to the Titty Twister is pounded on from the outside.

The vamps look towards it in horror.

From the other side of the door, we hear a voice with a Spanish accent.

VOICE
(*off screen; in Spanish*)
I'm looking for my friend. Is Seth in there?

Seth's face lights up like Rome burning.

SETH
(*yelling*)
Carlos!
(*in Spanish*)
Help us, bash the door in. Bash the door in!

CARLOS
(*off-screen; in Spanish*)
Danny, Manny, knock down the door. Hurry, hurry!

The vamps are totally fucking freaked out! They run and fly around the bar in a panic. Crying, howling, grabbing onto each other.

The front door is torn apart from shotgun fire coming from the outside, punching holes the size of basketballs in the door.

The table in front of the door gives and falls forward.

The door caves in and sunlight invades the bar. Many vamps are instantly fried, bursting into flames.

The Mexican gangster Carlos and his two henchmen, Danny and Manny, are horrified at what they see. They cross themselves in fright.

Vampires search for dark corners, but all is lost. Sunlight hits a mirrored ball attached to the ceiling, sending hundreds of beams of sunlight scattering through the room. Vamps try and dodge the beams. No dice. All around the bar vamps combust in fiery explosions.

The Titty Twister is now on fire, burning out of control.

Seth and Kate run through the burning building and leap through the door into the parking lot.

EXT. TITTY TWISTER PARKING LOT – MORNING

Carlos, Danny and Manny help them to their feet and walk them away from the blazing bar. They catch their breath by Carlos's Mercedes.

> CARLOS
> (*to Seth*)
What the fuck was going on in there?

Seth signals Carlos to wait a minute while he catches his breath. Then he hauls off and punches Carlos square in the kisser. Danny and Manny aim their shotguns at Seth.

CARLOS
(in Spanish)
Whatsamatter with you? Are you crazy?

SETH
Why the fuck, outta all the godforsaken shitholes in Mexico, did
you have us rendezvous at that place?

CARLOS
I don't know, one place's as good as another.

SETH
Have you ever been there before?

CARLOS
No, but I passed by it a couple of times. It's out in the middle of
nowhere. It seems like a rowdy place, so there wouldn't be a lot of
police. And it's open from dusk till dawn. You said meet you in
the morning.

SETH
Well, because you picked that place out of a hat, my brother's
dead now. And this girl's family's dead.

Carlos stands up again.

CARLOS
I'm sorry to hear that. What were they, psychos?

SETH
Did they look like psychos? They were fuckin' vampires. Psychos
don't explode when sunlight hits 'em, I don't care how crazy they are.

*Danny and Manny react to the vampire news by crossing themselves
again.*

CARLOS
Oh, Seth, how can I ever make it up to you?

SETH
You can't, but fifteen percent instead of thirty for my stay at El
Ray is a good start.

CARLOS
Twenty-eight.

SETH

Jesus Christ, Carlos, my brother's dead and he's not coming back, and it's all your fault. Twenty.

They look at each other, then shake hands, saying in unison:

SETH/CARLOS
(*in Spanish*)

Twenty-five.

(*pause*)

Done!

They hug one another.

TIME CUT:

Trunk of Seth's new Porsche is opened. The suitcase full of money is placed inside.

CARLOS

Do you like the car?

SETH

It looks great, but I said like new. This is a '90.

CARLOS

But it is like new. It belonged to a friend of mine – drug dealer – only drove it fourteen times in five years. Swear to God. That's like new.

SETH

So do I just follow you?

CARLOS

Yeah, follow us.

SETH

Let's do it.

CARLOS
(*to Danny and Manny*)

Vamanos!

Carlos, Danny and Manny pile into Carlos's white Mercedes.

Seth, by his Porche, looks back at Kate.

Kate stands alone.

The whole desert seems between them.

So much to say . . . but no words.

                    SETH

I'm sorry.

                    KATE

Me too.

Long pause.

                    SETH

See ya.

                    KATE

Later.

Seth turns his back on her. Just as he opens the door, Kate says behind him:

                    (*off-screen*)

Seth.

Seth turns around.

You want some company?

Seth smiles.

                    SETH

Kate honey, I may be a bastard. But I'm not a fuckin' bastard.

He blows her a kiss across the desert.

She blows one back.

Seth's in his car and gone.

Kate turns around, faces the endless desert before her and begins her long walk home.

THEME OF MOVIE BEGINS POUNDING.

CREDITS

Miramax Films Presents

A Band Apart
In Association With
Los Hooligans Productions

A Robert Rodriguez Film

CAST
(*in order of appearance*)

TEXAS RANGER EARL MCGRAW	Michael Parks
PETE BOTTOMS	John Hawkes
SETH GECKO	George Clooney
RED-HEADED HOSTAGE	Heidi McNeal
RICHARD GECKO	Quentin Tarantino
BLONDE HOSTAGE	Aimee Graham
JACOB FULLER	Harvey Keitel
KATE FULLER	Juliette Lewis
SCOTT FULLER	Ernest Liu
OLD-TIMER	Marc Lawrence
HOSTAGE GLORIA HILL	Brenda Hillhouse
NEWSCASTER KELLY HOUGE	Kelly Preston
FBI AGENT STANLEY CHASE	John Saxon
BORDER GUARD	Cheech Marin
CHET PUSSY	Cheech Marin
TITTY TWISTER GUITARIST & VOCALIST	Tito Larriva
TITTY TWISTER SAXOPHONIST	Pete Atasanoff
TITTY TWISTER DRUMMER	Johnny Vatos Hernandez
RAZOR CHARLIE	Danny Trejo
BIG EMILIO	Ernest Garcia
DANNY THE WONDER PONY	Danny the Wonder Pony
SEX-MACHINE	Tom Savini
FROST	Fred Williamson
SANTANICO PANDEMONIUM	Salma Hayek
MOUTH VAMP VICTIM	Gino Crognale
SANTANICO VICTIM	Greg Nicotero

CARLOS	Cheech Marin
DANNY	Cristos
MANNY	Mike Moroff
BAR DANCERS	Michelle Berube
	Neena Bidasha
	Veena Bidasha
	Ungela Brockman
	Madison Clark
	Maria Diaz
	Rosalia Hayakawa
	Janine Jordae
	Jacque Lawson
	Houston Leigh
	Janie Liszewski
	Tia Texada
STUNT COORDINATOR	Steve Davison
STUNT PLAYERS	William Atwell
	Robin Bonaccorsi
	Robert F. Brown
	Troy T. Brown
	Michele Burkett
	William H. Burton
	Jennifer J. Caputo
	Samuel D'Auria
	Steve Davison
	Tim Davison
	Freddie Hice
	Ricardo Gaona
	Lance Gilbert
	Troy Gilbert
	Nadine Grycan
	Randall J. Hall
	Tom Harper
	Anita Hartshorn
	Ace Hatem
	Dana Hee
	Steve Holladay
	Billy H. Hooker
	Buddyjoe Hooker
	Thomas Huff
	Jeffrey Imada
	Matt Johnston

Henry Kingi
Billy (William) Lucas
Gary McLarty
Bennie Moore Jr.
Greg Nicotero
Hugh Aodh O'Brien
Marina A. Oviedo
Manny Perry
Chad Randall
Troy Robinson
Danny Rogers
Erik L. Rondell
Frank Torres
Timothy P. Trella
Scott Wilder
Spice Williams

MONSTERS Jon Fidele
Michael McKay
Jake McKinnon
Josh Patton
Walter Phelan
Wayne Toth
Henrik Von Ryzin

CREDITS

CASTING	Johanna Ray, C.S.A. & Elaine J. Huzzar
SPECIAL MAKEUP EFFECTS	Kurtzman, Nicotero & Berger EFX Group, Inc.
MUSIC	Graeme Revell
COSTUME DESIGNER	Graciela Mazón
PRODUCTION DESIGNER	Cecilia Montiel
EDITOR	Robert Rodriguez
DIRECTOR OF PHOTOGRAPHY	Guillermo Navarro
CO-PRODUCERS	Elizabeth Avellán
	Paul Hellerman
	Robert Kurtzman
	John Esposito
EXECUTIVE PRODUCERS	Lawrence Bender
	Robert Rodriguez
	Quentin Tarantino

STORY	Robert Kurtzman
SCREENPLAY	Quentin Tarantino
PRODUCERS	Gianni Nunnari
	Meir Teper
DIRECTOR	Robert Rodriguez
PRODUCTION MANAGER	Paul Hellerman
POST-PRODUCTION SUPERVISOR	Tamara Smith
VISUAL EFFECTS SUPERVISORS	Dan Fort
	Elizabeth Avellán
	Diana Dru Botsford
1ST ASSISTANT DIRECTOR	Douglas Aarniokoski
2ND ASSISTANT DIRECTOR	Brian Bettwy
2ND 2ND ASSISTANT DIRECTOR	Dieter 'Dietman' Busch
PRODUCTION ACCOUNTANT	Steve Beeson
ASSISTANT ACCOUNTANT	Cheryl 'Venus' Ventura
ACCOUNTING ASSISTANT	Daniel Myers Boone
PRODUCTION COORDINATOR	Dawn Todd
ASST. PRODUCTION COORDINATOR	Cathy Agcayab
PRODUCTION SECRETARY	Jeff Swafford
KEY OFFICE PRODUCTION	Laura 'Captain' Rush
ASSISTANTS	John Patrick Hardin
SCRIPT SUPERVISOR	Lou Ann Quast
LOCATION MANAGER	Robert E. Craft
LOCATION ASSISTANTS	Kyle Oliver
	Douglas Dresser
CAMERA OPERATOR	Robert Rodriguez
CAMERA OPERATOR	Guillermo Navarro
1ST ASSISTANT CAMERA	Ziad Doueiri
1ST ASSISTANT CAMERA	Alan Cohen
2ND ASSISTANT CAMERA	Timothy Kane
2ND ASSISTANT CAMERA	Camille R. Freer
STEADICAM OPERATOR	Robert Rodriguez
ADD'L STEADICAM OPERATOR	David Chameides
FILM LOADER	David E. Berryman
CAMERA INTERN	Patrick Tackett
PRODUCTION SOUND MIXER	Mark Ulano
BOOM OPERATORS	Patrushkha Mierzwa
	Gloria Cooper
SOUND INTERN	Chris Sposa
KEY HAIR/MAKE-UP ARTIST	Ermahn Ospina
ASSISTANT HAIR/MAKE-UP	Don Malot
ASSISTANTS MAKE-UP	Heidi Grotsky

128

	Deborah Noelle Thurin
TATTOO ARTIST	Gill Montie
COSTUME SUPERVISOR	Jacqueline Aronson
ASSISTANT TO COSTUME DESIGNER	Britt Thorpe Sherwood
SET COSTUMER	Jillian Kreiner
COSTUMER	C. Houston Sams
SET COSTUMER ASSISTANT	Ireri Mazon
WARDROBE INTERN	Nathan Easterling
GAFFER	David Lee
BEST BOY ELECTRIC	Andrew T. Watts
	Nathan Hathaway
ELECTRICIANS	Heather Hillmeyer
	Flint Ellsworth
	Lennon Bass, Jr.
KEY GRIP	Rick Stribling
BEST BOY GRIP	James B. 'Crash' Irons
	Tim 'Stuffy' Soronen
DOLLY GRIP	Bob Ivanjack
GRIPS	Jason 'Jake' Crosss
	Vance Cohen
	Jeremy Launais
GRIP INTERN	Bryan Swerling
ART DIRECTOR	Mayne Schuyler Berke
SET DECORATOR	Felipe Fernandez del Paso
LEAD MAN	Chris Carriveau
SET DESIGNER	Colin de Rouin
PROPERTY MASTERS	Steve Joyner
	Caylah Eddlebluthe
ASSISTANT PROPERTY MASTER	Martin Milligan
SPECIAL WEAPONS DESIGNER	Steve Joyner
ON-SET DRESSER	McPherson O'Reilly Downs
BUYER	Jennie Harris
ART DEPARTMENT COORDINATOR	Abigail Sheiner
SET DRESSERS	Ken Carriveau
	Gregg M. Hartman
	Michael Whetstone
	Jeff Hay
	Paul Dowler
	Howard P. Miller
SWING GANG	Steven Ingrassia
	Michael J. Brady
	Ronald Russom

	Christine Gebele
ASSISTANT ART DIRECTOR	Adam Lustig
ASSISTANT SET DECORATOR	Mary Patvaldnieks
ART DEPT. PRODUCTION ASSISTANT	Melissa L. Hale
ART DEPT. INTERNS	Beto Casillas
	Amy Montgomery
	Jennifer Martinez
	Adam Nagel
CONSTRUCTION COORDINATOR	Brian Markey
CONSTRUCTION FOREMAN	Michael Atwell
LEAD CARPENTER	Shane Hawkins
CONSTRUCTION ESTIMATOR	Chris Scher
LEAD SCENIC	Marco Gillson
SCENIC CARPENTERS	Chris Barnes
	Colin Bardon
	James M. Drury
	Bruce Harris
	Shawn Hawkins
	Mark Peters
	Ramsey Smith
	James Stanberry
	Floyd R. Valero
ON-SET CARPENTER	Scot Cummings
PAINTERS	James C. Beeson
	Jennifer Flynn
	Wendy Jerde
	Adam Markey
	Pedro V. Suchite
	Carlos A. Chavez
LABORER	Oswaldo Rojas
SCULPTORS	Alex Bogartz
	Bob Clark
	Larry E. McCauley
	David Shwartz
TITTY TWISTER SIGN BY	Gerald Martinez
IST ASSISTANT EDITOR	Daniel A. Fort
ASSISTANT EDITORS	Ethan Maniquis
	Joaquin G. Avellán
MUSIC EDITOR	Joshua Winget
MUSIC CONSULTANTS	Mary Ramos
	Chuck Kelley

DIALOGUE COACH FOR MR KEITEL	Jon Sperry
UNIT PUBLICIST	Katherine Moore & Associates
UNIT STILL PHOTOGRAPHER	Joyce Rudolph
CASTING ASSISTANT	Mary Jane Lavacca
EXTRAS CASTING BY	Rainbow Casting
ASSISTANT TO MR BENDER	Courtney McDonnell
ASSISTANT TO MR RODRIGUEZ	Mark Thornhill
ASSISTANT TO MR TARANTINO	Victoria Lucai
ASSISTANT TO MR CLOONEY	Amy Minda Cohen
ASSISTANT TO MR KEITEL	Loren Lockwood
ASSISTANT TO CO-PRODUCERS	Corinne T. Needle
KEY SET PRODUCTION ASSISTANT	Ben Parker
SET PRODUCTION ASSISTANTS	Jay Y. Beattie
	Teresa Delucio
	Aaron Penn
OFFICE PRODUCTION INTERNS	Geoff Hale
	Lowell Northrop
	Peri Silverman
MAKE-UP FX SUPERVISORS	Robert Kurtzman
	Greg Nicotero
	Howard Berger
MAKE-UP FX DESIGNER/ ILLUSTRATOR	John Bisson
MAKE-UP FX COORDINATOR	Kamar Bitar
MAKE-UP FX SHOP FOREMAN	Shannon Shea
MAKE-UP FX KEY PERSONNEL	Gino Crognale
	Wayne Toth
	Norman Cabrera
	Christopher Robbins
	Henrik Van Ryzin
SCULPTORS	Mark Alfrey
	Evan Campbell
	Mark Tavares
	Greg Smith
MOLDMAKERS	Mike McCarty
	Eric Harris
	Alan Tuskes
MECHANICS	Jeff Edwards
	Jake McKinnon
	Luke Khanlian
	Hiroshi Ikeuchi
	Mario Castillo

	Larry Odien
	David Kindlon
LAB TECHNICIANS	Brian Rae
	John Fidele
	Ted Hainee
	David Wogh
	Nick Marra
	Gary Jones
	Rob Hinderstein
	William Hunt
	Rodd Matsui
	Scott 'Goody' Goudreau
	Jason 'Junior' McCord
	Mack 'The Knife' McInville
	'Lonesome' George Nadian
	Tom 'The Switch' O'Donnell
	Geoff 'T-Bone' Teagardin
	Earl 'Mr Blonde' Thielen
	Tracy 'Ace' Thielen
STAND-INS	William Atwell
	Pam Rosenberg
MEDIC/STAGE MANAGER	Taylor A. Cummings
STUDIO TEACHER	Jan D. Tys
SET SECURITY BY	Technical Guard Security,
	Nick Roberts, Supervisor
PRODUCTION CATERING BY	Mario's Catering
CRAFT SERVICE	Ken Bondy
CRAFT SERVICE ASSISTANT	Andrew T. Rothmund
A BAND APART LEGAL	Carlos Goodman (Lichter,
	Grossman & Nichols, Inc.)
LOS HOOLIGANS LEGAL	Craig Emanuel (Sinclair,
	Tenenbaum & Olesiuk)
MUSIC LEGAL SERVICES	Myman, Abell, Fineman,
	Greenspan & Rowan
LABOR ATTORNEY	Richard W. Kopenhefer
INSURANCE PROVIDERS	Great Northern/Reiff & Associates
COMPLETION GUARANTORS	Film Finances, Inc., Kurt Woolner
	& Maureen Duffy
SNAKES PROVIDED BY	Reptile Rentals
TRAINER	Jules Sylvester
DOGS PROVIDED BY	Cougar Hill Ranch
TRAINERS	Nicholas Toth

132

Chandra Marrs

Alvin Mears

VIDEO PLAYBACK PROVIDED BY Playback Technologies

VISUAL EFFECTS PHOTOGRAPHY

VISUAL EFFECTS DIRECTOR Diana Dru Botsford

SCRIPT SUPERVISOR Rochelle Gross

1ST ASSISTANT DIRECTOR David Vincent Rimer

DIRECTOR OF PHOTOGRAPHY James Belkin

ASSISTANT CAMERA Rudy Pahoyo

Gary Anderton

GAFFER Eric S. Foster

ADDITIONAL GAFFER Briant T. Louks

KEY GRIP John Warner

ADDITIONAL KEY GRIP Kevin Wadowski

GRIPTRICIAN Jose Ricardo 'Stick Shift' Martinez

Taylor Sparks

Jason Elias

VIDEO EFFECTS SWITCHER

OPERATOR Jeff Burrage

PRODUCTION ASSISTANTS Jack M. Harvey

Nicole Hearon

Todd Lincoln

ADDITIONAL PHOTOGRAPHY – MEXICO UNIT

UNIT PRODUCTION MANAGER Luz Maria Rojas

FIRST ASSISTANT CAMERA Gerardo Manjarrez

PRODUCTION ASSISTANTS Tommy Nix

Dan Shaw

VISUAL EFFECTS COORDINATOR Rochelle Gross

PRE-VISUALIZATION ARTIST Gina Warr

DIGITAL IMAGERY/COMPOSITING BY THE POST GROUP

EXECUTIVE PRODUCER OF VISUAL

FX Mark Franco

CREATIVE DIRECTOR/SR DIGITAL

COMPOSITOR Peter Sternlicht

DIGITAL COMPOSITOR Steve Scott

VISUAL FX PRODUCER Karen Skouras

DIGITAL FILM SCANNING &

RECORDING Christopher Kutcha

DIGITAL DATA COORDINATOR Linda Cordella

DIGITAL SYSTEMS ENGINEER Joe Davenport

VISUAL FX ANIMATOR Genevieve Yee

VISUAL FX ANIMATOR	Julie Glazer
VISUAL FX TRAINEE	Ahryn Scott

CGI BAT VISUAL EFFECTS BY VIFX

Rhonda C. Gunner, Richard E. Hollander, Gregory L. McMurry, John C. Wash

VISUAL FX SUPERVISOR	John C. Wash
VISUAL FX PRODUCER	Josh R. Jaggars
DIGITAL SUPERVISOR	John (D. J.) Desjardin
3D CGI SUPERVISOR	Antoine Durr
ANIMATOR	Morris May
SIMULATION SOFTWARE	Andy Kopra
DIGITAL COMPOSITING SUPERVISOR	Cheryl Budgett
2ND TEAM	Tony Diep
	Harry Lam
	Edwin Rivera
	Gregory Ellwood
ART DIRECTOR/MATTE ARTIST	Karen Dejong

CUSTOM 3D BAT DATASETS PROVIDED BY VIEWPOINT DATALABS INTERNATIONAL

MATTE PAINTING BY ILLUSION ARTS, INC.

VISUAL EFFECTS SUPERVISOR	Robert Stromberg
PRODUCTION MANAGER	Catherine Sudolcan
MATTE PHOTOGRAPHY	Mark Sawicki
DIGITAL MATTE ARTIST	Mike Wassel
MATTE EFFECTS	Lynn Ledgerwood
POST-PRODUCTION ACCOUNTANT	Cheryl 'Venus' Ventura
POST-PRODUCTION ASSISTANTS	Laura 'Captain' Rush
SUPERVISING SOUND EDITOR	Dean Beville
SOUND EDITORS	Gregory Hedgepath
	Charles Ewing Smith
	Charles Maynes
	Patricio Liebenson
	Allan Bromberg
DIALOGUE EDITOR	Frank Smathers
SUPERVISING ADR EDITOR	Harry Miller III
ADR EDITOR	Beth Bergeron
FOLEY EDITORS	Scott Curtis
	Solange Boisseau
FOLEY WALKERS	Sean Rowe
	Laura Macias

SOUND RECORDIST	Matt Beville
ASSISTANT SOUND EDITOR	Dana Gustafson
APPRENTICE SOUND EDITOR	Thomas Fabricante
	Bob Wishnefsky
ADR/FOLEY RECORDIST	Dana Porter
ADR/FOLEY MIXER	Robert Deschaine, C.A.S.
RE-RECORDING FACILITIES	Twentieth Century Fox
	Sound Department
RE-RECORDING MIXERS	Sergio Reyes
	Tennyson Sebastian II
	Robert Rodriguez
	Thomas P. Gerard
DUBBING RECORDIST	Tim Gomillion
LOADER	Carrie Minkler
STAGE ENGINEER	Gary W. Carlson
DUBBING PROJECTIONIST	John Bates
COLOR TIMER	David Orr
NEGATIVE CUTTER	Mo Henry
DOLBY STEREO CONSULTANT	Thom 'Coach' Ehle

ORIGINAL MOTION PICTURE SOUNDTRACK AVAILABLE
ON EPIC CDS AND CASSETTES

Special Thanks To:
Adidas
Robert Blake
Hugo Boss
(Anheuser-Busch) Budweiser
Caterpillar, Inc.
Cinema One Spectrum
Converse
Fat Dog and Raider
Joel Fitzpatrick
Brian Gersh
George Gomez
Craig Hammon
Harley Davidson
Icee
Keds
Sheldon Lettich
Mossimo Women
Robert Newman
Nike

Claudia Ortiz
PCL
Place It Entertainment
Salvador Quiroz
Teresa Rodriguez
Rona
Salvation Navy
Diego Sandoval
Mike Simpson
Snack King
Jim Thompson
Turtle Beach
UPP
John Wells
Jim Wilson

Special Thanks to the Cities of Barstow and Lancaster
and Scott Spiegel

Stock Footage provided by
Film & Video Stock Shorts

Gripp and Electric Equipment provided by
Hollywood Rentals

Cameras provided by
Otto Nemenz

Camera Dolly provided by
J. L. Fisher, Inc.

Titles & Opticals by
Cinema Research Corporation

Originated on Eastman Color Negative

Color by
Technicolor

SDDS

DOLBY ® SR
in Selected Theaters